ONEGAI ✳ TWINS 🏠

2 ✳ A PAIR AND ONE ✳

GO ZAPPA

Illustrations by Taraku Uon & Hiroaki Gohda
Original Work by Please!

Contents

ONEGAI TWINS

2 * A PAIR AND ONE *

Translator
Gretchen Kern

Editors
Shawn Sanders
Kevin P. Croall

Production Artist
Anya Lin

US Cover Design
Yuki Chung

Production Manager
Janice Chang

Art Director
Yuki Chung

Marketing
Nicole Curry

President
Robin Kuo

© GO ZAPPA
© Pleasel / Bandai Visual

First published in 2004 by
Media Works Inc., Tokyo, Japan.
English translation rights arranged with
Media Works Inc.

ONEGAI TWINS NOVEL v2
English translation © 2004
ComicsOne, Corp.
All rights reserved.

Publisher
ComicsOne Corporation
48531 Warm Springs Blvd., #408
Fremont, CA 94539
www.ComicsOne.com

First Edition: September 2004
ISBN 1-58899-002-8

ONEGAI ✳ TWINS

2 ✳ A PAIR AND ONE ✳

Chapter 7: Wild Vacation

After finishing his lunch, Maiku Kamishiro relaxed in his own seat in the classroom. Just then, without any lead-in, Kosei Shimazaki said, "...and that's why I think we should go to the beach together next weekend, Maiku," and pulled out an envelope tied with red and white string.

"Wait a minute!"

Despite normal appearances, this classmate's brain was full of weird ideas, and although he should have been used to his crazy outbursts, this came as a surprise.

"That's why!? What's why?"

"This is."

Kosei, with an attitude suggesting that he thought it was Maiku's problem for not being able to follow the conversation, waved the envelope in front of his face. Maiku, overwhelmed by Kosei's intensity, fell back in his chair.

"What's that?"

"It's an invitation for your family of four to enjoy one night and two days at the beach. I won it yesterday from a drawing at the supermarket in front of the train station."

Kosei retracted his hand holding the envelope, turned his head and smiled.

"Well, I guess this shows that I've got good luck."

If that's true, then God's eye-sight must be getting really bad in his old age.

"Then why do I have to go with you?" Maiku asked innocently, but Kosei looked at him as if to say, 'You just don't get it,' and replied, "It would be boring to go alone."

"Alone...? It's an invitation for a family of four. Why don't you go with your family?"

"That's what I had in mind, but for some reason, no one wants to go with me."

"I see."

Maiku felt a little bad for him, but Kosei's family members were only human. It wasn't that hard to understand. "I think I know how your family feels."

"Don't you?"

You shouldn't be so happy about it, Maiku thought to say, but kept this biting remarks to himself.

"So here's where you come in, Maiku."

"But why me?"

"Oh, Maiku, you shouldn't have to ask!"

Kosei gave him a lewd look and Maiku replied curtly, "I'm not psychic!"

"Hey! If that ticket's for a family of four, that means two more people can go to the beach with you!" Miina Miyafuji jumped into the conversation, appearing suddenly out of nowhere. Surprised, Maiku turned to the direction of the voice and saw Karen Onodera peeking out from behind Miina.

"When did you guys get here?"

"Well, let's not worry about the details," Miina said, waving her hand up and down as if she was fanning Maiku.

Karen nodded saying, "If we must say, it was an action based on the expanded interpretation of the fifth code of our love alliance."

"Huh? Alliance? Code?" Maiku furrowed his brow at the unfamiliar words and Miina nervously elbowed Karen in the side.

"Nothing... nothing at all."

The "Love Alliance Code" that Karen carelessly let slip referred to the agreement concerning the love alliance that she and Miina made. They made these agreements during a conversation in the bathtub which lasted until they grew dizzy. Those agreements are as follows:

Love Alliance Code

1. Until we know for sure which of us is related by blood to Maiku, neither of us shall confess our love to him.

2. If one of us finds out that she is related by blood to Maiku, she will immediately tell the other.

3. The one who is related by blood to Maiku will support a relationship between Maiku and the non-related party.

4. If any other girl tries to approach Maiku, we will work together so she cannot get close to him.

5. We will stay with Maiku.

Further explanation of the fifth code, "we will stay with Maiku" means, they would continue living with Maiku as they had been, without anyone leaving on their own. It did not mean that they would stay glued to him constantly, just to remain as a family. However, Karen and Miina expanded the interpretation, and having just finished lunch, they came from their classroom next door to glue themselves to Maiku. No matter what you may think of someone who reinterprets the rules they make up themselves, the two girls believed that their rule-bending was allowed because it was permissible to dispatch troops to a foreign country even while constitutionally declaring surrender. That said, the lunchtime visits to Maiku's classroom also doubled as an information-gathering practice. If any other girl, particularly the second year student, Tubaki Oribe, who Miina called "Hoochie girl with glasses", tried to get in the way, the fourth code would immediately go into effect, and they would use the full extent of their abilities to remove the obstacle. Fortunately, it had never reached that level of danger, but for Maiku who had intended on brusquely refusing Kosei's invitation, the two girls had come at a very bad time.

"Anyway, umm…" said Miina trailing off as she realized she did not know the name of the person she was trying to speak to.

"My name is Kosei Shimazaki," said Kosei, realizing the reason for the pause. "I have a very deep relationship with Maiku-ie."

"Hey!" said Maiku in protest, but Miina ignored this.

"Well then, Shimazaki."

"We're friends, call me Charlie!" pronounced Kosei, puzzlingly.

After a brief hesitation Karen asked, "Um, why Charlie, if your last name is Shimazaki?"

"Because my first name is Kosei." Karen, Miina, and Maiku stared at him with looks of blank confusion at his random comment. Kosei seemed unconcerned. In general, he was not use to not being understood.

"Well, let's just forget about names for now," said Miina, having somehow recovered. "If you don't know anyone besides Maiku to go with you, could we come along, too?"

This was just the kind of deeply-rooted impudence one might expect from the girl who had insisted on moving in with someone she had never met. Had she not been speaking to someone as crazy as Kosei, Maiku might have chided Miina for being so forward.

"You wanna come too?"

"Um, if possible, I would like to come as well," Karen said taking a half step forward. She certainly did not want to be left behind.

"Hmmm...." Kosei thought for a while, but finally turned to Maiku and asked, "What do you think, Maiku? Should we take them with us?"

"Well, since I didn't even wanna go..."

"What!? Why not?"

Miina pouted and her disbelief showed on her face.

"Let's gooo! He was nice enough to invite us along on his free trip!"

"That's right, Maiku! We don't get many chances like this!" Karen added, also excited about going.

"So that's how it is. Maiku won't go with me." Kosei's head drooped pointedly towards his chest and eyed Miina and Karen through a gap in the bangs which hung over his face. "That's too bad. I would have taken these two girls with us if only Maiku had agreed to go along."

"Maiku!"

"Maiku-san!"

Miina and Karen spoke together, as if by reflex.

"Are you going to spoil our summer vacation with your selfishness?"

"Yes! That's cruel!"

"Hold on. You're playing right into Kosei's plan!"

Miina and Karen had fallen for Kosei's transparent gimmick, and could not be swayed to heed Maiku's warning.

"So Maiku thinks we're a nuisance. That we're good-for-nothing freeloaders who don't deserve to enjoy their summers like everyone else."

"Waah. That's so mean!"

"Don't cry, Karen. Such is our sorry fate. We will never lay in the sand, bath in the bright light of the sun, nor spend the hot summer days slurping cold noodles from last year as is the destiny of those with a shady past," Miina said, as the movements from her performance lead her over to Karen's side, who still looked close to tears.

"What's going on? Did they have a fight with Maiku?"

"Dunno, but those girls look like they're crying."

"What? A lover's spat?"

Their classmates, who were sensing trouble and had gathered in the back of the classroom, now began whispering secretly while shooting curious glances toward the front. This was the situation Maiku most wanted to avoid. He made a sour face and, not caring about it, Karen finally began to cry. In a voice loud enough for everyone around them to hear, Miina shouted, "Don't cry, Karen. Forget about it. Summer won't come for us."

"Waaah. Farewell, modest happiness."

"Fine! We'll go!" Maiku said out of desperation.

Kosei lifted his head and said, "You'll go with me, Maiku-ie!"

"Aah!" Maiku shrieked, finding Kosei's arms suddenly wrapped around him.

"Yay! We're going to the beach!"

"Yes! The beach! A vacation!"

Karen and Miina held hands and jumped around in a circle.

"Well that worked out nicely."

"You mean that it was settled because Kamishiro and Shimazaki are so close?"

"Um, well..."

Imagining what his listening classmates must have thought, Maiku sighed deeply, still being hugged by Kosei.

"Oh, look! It's the ocean!" Miina said in a cheerful voice, pointing at the ocean, shimmering against the July sun. It had just come into view as the train pulls out of the tunnel. In the seat beside her, Karen turns toward the opened window, the sea air blowing through her long hair. She looks out to the ocean with sparkling eyes.

"Wow! I can't believe how beautiful it is!"

Maiku, sitting next to Kosei which is across from the girls, had the same sullen look on his face that they'd come to expect.

"Come on, you're not kids anymore. You don't have to get so excited about it. It makes you look stupid."

By the time the local train left the mountains, heading for the Sea of Japan, it was pretty vacant, and Maiku, Miina, Karen, and Kosei had the car almost entirely to themselves.

"Oh, let them be! It's nice to see them so happy," Kosei said, peeling a tangerine he bought at a kiosk before near the train station. "We can look after them and pretend they are our children."

"No amount of imagination would make that possible," Maiku spat out the words.

He was wearing a black polo shirt with culottes. Kosei wore a sleeveless shirt that was perfectly fitted to his body, tight over the waist so over his military pants. He held one segment of his peeled tangerine between two fingers and moved it toward Maiku's mouth.

"Say 'ah,' Maiku-ie."

"You're not feeding me!"

"Aw, you're embarrassed."

"I am not!"

"Oh, would you rather take it from my mouth?"

"Idiot."

Karen watched this exchange from her seat across from them and leaned over to Miina's ear to whisper, "Miina, would something like this fall under code four?"

"Hard to say."

The fourth code of their Love Alliance was "If any other girls try to approach Maiku, we will work together so they cannot get close to him." Kosei wasn't a girl, of course, but the girls, both of whom loved Maiku, could not stand to by with this flirting.

"What should we do?"

"For the moment, let's just watch and see how things go."

Miina and Karen both seemed to think it would not be right to be cruel to Kosei, after all, it was he who had been nice enough to invite them along on this trip.

"We must believe Maiku's interests are decent."

"Can we believe that?"

"Of course you can!" Maiku yelled, spit flying. He had over-heard the girls' secret conversation.

At that, Kosei nodded. "That's right! You don't have to worry. Maiku will return my love!"

"That's not what I meant!"

Just then, the train reached its destination and the doors opened with a sigh. Miina was the first out the door, with her bulging sports bag slung over one shoulder. Next was Kosei, followed by Maiku, and last was Karen, tottering under an old-fashioned trunk. It looked like they were the only ones getting off at the stop. There didn't seem to be anyone inside the station, but plastic lanterns with letters painted on them spelling out "W E L C O M E" hung from a wire stretched between two poles. They had not been expecting much from a trip won in a raffle, but for a tourist location it looked pretty desolate indeed. But Miina and Karen, who were happy enough just to be going to the beach with Maiku, bounded towards the ticket gate. They raced through the station which, perhaps because of long exposure to the salty wind, was noticeably rusty. Miina wore a deacon blue sleeveless shirt and yellow miniskirt, and Karen wore a camisole that looked as if it could have been dyed in ripe watermelon juice, over a pair of slim hemp pants. Bright light shone down from the cloudless sky onto the two girls. They were openly excited about this one day vacation.

"Where do we go now?" Maiku said as he stepped out of the ticket gate last, squinting in the bright light.

Kosei looked around and said, "There should be a car from the inn to pick us up."

"Hey!" Maiku and Kosei turned in the direction of the voice and saw a man waving his arm. He was standing next to a white van parked a short distance from the station. He looked to be about forty years old. He appeared powerfully built and was wearing a blue Hawaiian shirt. The man walked over to them and said, "You must be here to stay at the Godai Inn."

"Er..." Maiku seemed unable to reply, but Kosei took the note from his pocket and checked the name of the inn.

"That's right. I'm Shimazaki. My reservation is under the name 'Charlie.'"

"Right. Well, I've brought the car. Please come this way."

"The car's over this way," Maiku beckoned to Miina and Karen, wondering why Kosei had used the name Charlie.

As soon as the two ran up to them, the man in the Hawaiian shirt lead them to the van with "Godai Inn" lettered on its side. Kosei sat in the front and Maiku sat between Miina and Karen in the second row of seats behind. The man in the Hawaiian shirt closed the door from the outside, climbed into the driver's seat and started the engine.

"Here we go."

Just as the van began to move, a hand reached up from the back seats and grabbed Maiku's shoulder.

"Fancy meeting you here, Kamishiro."

Maiku turned around, surprised, and saw Tubaki Oribe smiling at him. She was wearing a white tank top coordinated with a custard-colored skirt made of thin material. A gold, heart-shaped pendant glittered at her throat.

"Ms. Oribe!" What are you doing here?" Maiku was at a loss for words over this unexpected meeting, but the student council president,

Ichigo Morino, responded in a monotonous voice.

"It's the student council secret retreat."

"You're here too, Ms. President!"

Even though it was summer, Ichigo was wearing a short sleeved black dress trimmed with lace at the hem. It looked like something one might wear home from a funeral. Miina and Karen, like Maiku, were not ready with replies to this unexpected coincidence. Even Kosei, who had stuck his head out from behind the passenger seat, was wide-eyed.

Maiku finally recovered from his shock enough to ask, "What do you do at a student council secret retreat?"

Ichigo replied with a serious look, "It's a secret retreat, so that information is secret."

"I... see."

"If you really want to know, you can come find me later. I'll tell you privately."

"No, that's quite all right." He felt somehow it was better not to know and refused Ichigo's invitation.

When they had driven about fifteen minutes down the unpaved road, leaving a cloud of dust behind them, the inn came into sight. The log building looked fairly old, and if they had been told it was built during the Edo Period, they would have believed it.

"Here we are." The driver parked the van in front of the inn and jumped out of the driver's seat. After opening the door from the outside, he turned to face the open door of the inn and announced, "Mr. Charlie's party and the Kizaki High School Student Council Leaders have arrived."

Maiku and his group could not have said anything about the manner of their announcement, but Ichigo and Tubaki had picked a rather pretentious name for themselves. Everyone got out of the car, and after stretching from their short drive, saw two figures making their way to the inn from the nearby bus stop.

"Hm? Who are you...?"

The group, now six, including Ichigo and Tubaki, turned together in the direction of the voice. Matagu Shido was walking in front and he spotted Ichigo.

"Even Morino's here."

An uncharacteristic look of open disgust showed on Ichigo's face, barely visible in the group.

"What's going on? Why are you guys all here?"

"That's what I'd like to know!" Ichigo said, and Matagu, in a T-shirt and knee-length shorts, turned to look at the inn, which looked like it could be brought to the ground by one shake of an earthquake.

"Some distant relations of mine run this place. I came to spend the night."

"A coincidence planned by the devil himself!"

"So, Morino, why are you...?"

"Oh, Miina and Karen!" Haruko called out happily, cutting off her brother's words. Running up to them she said, "Wow! I never thought I'd see you here!"

Haruko, in a sleeveless top and tiny jean shorts, grabbed Miina and Karen's hands and beamed at them so brightly they were at a loss. "I'm so glad you're here! I woulda been bored to tears all alone with my brother!"

At this, Matagu's mouth twitched noticeably.

"Let's all have lots of fun together!"

"Thank you for waiting, sirs and madams." A small old woman stepped out of the entrance, and wiping her hands on her apron as if she had just pulled herself away from an important task. In her round-necked shirt and traditional Japanese women's work pants, the old woman seemed well-suited to the building.

"Grandma Godai!"

"Ohh!" As soon as she saw Matagu, she opened her eyes that had at once seemed buried in wrinkles. It was an excited expression that was soon replaced by one of suspicion.

"Who were you again?"

Matagu, who had started walking towards the old woman with his arms outstretched, could not help feeling a little foolish.

"Come on, it's me! Matagu, from Nagano! How could you forget?"

"Hah hah hah! I'm just kidding. You were always fun to tease." She laughed with great pleasure at her now desperate relation. "So, are all these people your friends?"

"Yeah," Matagu nodded. "This is my classmate, Morino, and these are my dear underclassmen."

Miina, Karen, and Tubaki made faces in unison at being referred to as a group of his "dear underclassmen." Because it was the unavoidable truth, it seemed difficult for the teenage girls to put up with being thought of only as Matagu's underclassmen.

"Really." She nodded slightly and turned to the others, now all lumped into one group. "Thanks for coming. There's nothing here but the beach, but I hope you have a nice stay."

They somehow felt more like they'd come to visit relatives,

instead of coming to stay at an inn on vacation.

"Well then..." The man in the Hawaiian shirt, who seemed to be an employee of the inn, hopped into the van, and sticking his head out the driver's side window said, "Right then, granny, I'm gonna take the car around back."

"All right, thanks."

The van pulled onto a small road that ran along side the inn, and the old lady led her guests into the open doorway of the inn.

"Right this way, please."

The inside of the inn smelled like dry wood as they followed the old lady up a flight of creaking stairs.

"First, the group of two can stay here." The old lady opened the sliding door of the first room at the top of the stairs and showed Ichigo and Tubaki inside. She came back out immediately, and showed Maiku to the neighboring room.

"This will be for the four of you." The room they were shown was a Japanese-style room big enough to hold eight tatami mats. In the middle of the room sat a heavy-looking low table. Just like the building itself, the tatami mats showed their age. They were a size larger than modern ones and had all been bleached from constant exposure to the sun. The windows opened up to a good view of the blue ocean, letting in a cool sea breeze.

"Wow!" Miina and Karen exclaimed their appreciation for the view.

"The beach is really close," Miina said.

"There's nothing else here, so make sure you swim as much as you like," the old lady responded, getting things ready for tea.

"Come on! Let's go swimming right away!" Miina seemed ready to change into her swimsuit that very instant.

"Calm down a minute! First put down your bags and settle down!" Maiku said frowning. Just then, the sliding door connecting their room to the one beside it opened and Tubaki stuck her head in.

"So they are connected by a sliding door."

It appeared the rooms were identical.

"Grandma, can I stay up here with everyone else?" Haruko called from the hallway, waiting for the old lady to finish up her work. She finished preparing the tea and spoke.

"No, these rooms are for the customers, so you and...."

"It's Matagu, grandma!" Thinking she had forgotten his name, Matagu supplied it.

"Oh, right, right. You and Matagu should be with me, in another part of the inn."

"I don't mind if she stays with us," Tubaki said and looked at Ichigo, who was kneeling on the floor drinking tea. "That's all right with you too, isn't it, Ms. President?"

"It's fine. The room is too big for just the two of us. It would feel too empty."

"If you say so," the old lady said, though she did not seem convinced.

"All right!" Haruko threw both arms in the air in excitement.

"In that case, I think I'd rather stay here..." Matagu started. Tubaki's face stiffened. She had forgotten that Haruko's loser brother would want to come, if Haruko was allowed.

"Whaaat? Are you gonna stay here too, Matagu?"

Thinking nothing of the annoyance that showed so plainly on her face, Matagu responded decidedly, "Naturally. Siblings are of one mind and one body. Of course they should stay together." He added quickly after that, "And I don't mean "one mind, one body" in any sort of dirty way." Saying this did not have its intended effect and instead made it sound like her brother had accidentally revealed his secret desires. Haruko looked at him like she might look at a particularly disgusting insect.

"How about if we split the boys and girls into two separate rooms," Ichigo suggested quietly.

"That sounds great! We can make this the girls' room and that can be for the boys." Tubaki was quick to join in.

"What!!?" Miina and Karen voiced their dissatisfaction together at this sudden decision. "Why do you wanna do that?"

"Yes! I don't like it!"

"It'll be fine. There won't be any mistakes if we split up by gender," Tubaki said, and Miina snapped back with, "There won't be any mistakes anyway!"

"If you don't think you'll make any mistakes, then we should just separate the rooms anyway."

Miina was at a loss for words, and turned towards Maiku who was sipping over-steeped tea out of a chipped tea cup. "Maikuuu! Say something!"

"I think that Tubaki's idea is fine."

"Maiku!" Miina said in a shrill voice, while Karen, too shocked for anything else, drew in sharp breaths where she sat.

"It would be easier that way, when we have to change into swimsuits and such." Maiku said, looking away from Miina and Karen.

At that, Tubaki said in a pleased voice, "It's settled then."

"Shimazaki, are you all right with that?" Ichigo asked in a voice that carried surprisingly well, for how quietly she spoke.

"I don't care as long as I'm with Maiku."

"Have you made up your minds?" the old lady asked. She had been watching to see how things would turn out.

"Yes, the girls will stay here, and the boys will be over there," Ichigo said with a nod.

"Very well. I'm sorry to be a bother, but would you mind having Haruko and Matagi...."

"I said I'm Matagu!" Matagu protested, and the old lady bowed her head in apology. In response, Tubaki turned toward the old lady with her best smile and said, "Please don't worry about it. We'll have more fun if we're all together."

And so, the bedroom situation was finally decided, and the old lady left after having her guestbook signed, and Miina and Karen reluctantly moved their bags into the next room. In contrast to that gloomy looking pair, Haruko was in very good spirits.

"I'm so glad I get to stay with you, Miina and Karen! Let's hurry up and get changed so we can go to the beach!"

Miina and Karen knew it would do them no good to act like spoiled children, so they closed the sliding door between the rooms and got ready to go to the beach. While the other girls were pulling towels and swimsuits out of their bags, Miina quickly took off her shirt and miniskirt, revealing her school swimsuit and socks. She had left the house that morning with her swimsuit under her clothes.

Karen, who had just now taken off her hemp pants, widened her eyes in surprise at Miina's fast change. "You came ready, didn't you, Miina?"

"Yep," Miina said, puffing her chest out.

"Oh, come on! We're not elementary school students anymore, so don't act so childish!" Tubaki was down to her underwear, trying to unhook her bra with a hand behind her back. "Well, I guess childish behavior suits your childish figure."

"What did you say!?" Miina, who was quick to anger over comments on what was a very sensitive topic for her, responded with a look that evaded description. However, Tubaki was apparently unbothered by this, and, as if to bounce Miina's anger back at her, stood topless and said, "I can't believe anyone would come all the way to the ocean and wear their school swimsuit."

Living on Maiku's meager earnings, Miina and Karen did not have the kind of money that would allow them to buy new swimsuits just because they were going to the beach. Miina could not think of a reply to that, and bit her lip. Just then, Ichigo spoke up from the corner of the room, where she had been changing.

"Oh, I'm wearing my school swimsuit too."

"What?" Tubaki turned to look at Ichigo, now only wearing a pair of underpants, holding out a school swimsuit in her hands.

"It's the old one." The school swimsuit Ichigo held had wider straps than the one Miina was wearing and was of a less fashionable design.

"But why?" Tubaki made an unreadable face. She could hardly fathom Ichigo's intentions by purposefully bringing a swimsuit that was no longer used, rather than the one she used in gym class.

"I suppose you could call it an obsession."

Tubaki nodded, but looked like she'd missed the point, and continued changing into her swimsuit, dumbfounded.

"Whoa!"

As soon as they arrived at the beach, just five minutes away from the inn, Miina looked out at the waves pounding on the clean beach and let out her excitement. She pulled a towel and tanning oil out of her vinyl bag, kicked off her sandals and ran toward the water at full speed, like a dog on his first walk in a while. Behind her, wearing his school swim trunks for the same reason as the two free-loaders, Maiku called out, "Hey! Make sure you stretch first!"

Miina ran into the ocean, apparently deaf to Maiku's cry.

"It's like someone flipped a switch on her," Karen said, picking up the sandals and bag Miina dropped.

"Jeez," Maiku commented bitterly.

Either because it was still early in the season, or because it was somewhere no one but the locals visited, the beach was quiet. There was only one beach house there, and it looked like it could be blown away by one strong gust of wind. It was somewhat lonely, but they felt like they could relax and enjoy their time there.

Miina seemed satisfied after playing around in the shallows for a while, and came back to the resting place they had made by spreading a vinyl sheet on the beach and putting their bags on each of the four corners. Still out of breath, she grabbed Karen's hand and said, "Come on! What are you waiting around for? Let's go!"

"What? But I'm not ready yet..."

Miina dragged her to the water's edge.

"Um... Maiku said we should do warm-up stretches before we go in...."

"Don't be a drag. You can stretch after!"

"But then it wouldn't be warm-up stretches!"

While they were arguing, a big wave came and knocked Karen off her feet and onto her bottom.

"Eep!"

Karen scrambled away from the water, as if she were afraid of being dragged out to sea with the retreating waves. Miina watched this and asked, as the waves washed over her ankles once again, "Is this your first time coming to the ocean?"

Karen nodded, looking fearfully out at the open water. "There aren't sharks or anything, are there?"

"..."

Miina purposefully left a gap in the conversation. "There won't be any sharks here."

"You had to think about your answer a little, didn't you, Miina? Why?"

Miina looked away casually and Karen's face paled.

"There really are sharks here, aren't there!"

Miina burst into laughter and reached out to Karen, who had backed away from her. "A shark wouldn't come somewhere there was no food."

"Absolutely?"

"Yeah," Miina nodded. "There might be some twenty foot long

giant squid though."

"Aaah! That's even worse!"

While Miina teased Karen, Haruko ran up to them with an inner tube. In her red one-piece swimsuit with fluttering red trim, she looked just like a Chinese goldfish.

"Carpe diem!" Shouting this difficult phrase she'd learned from who knows where, Haruko lunged at them, and Miina and Karen fell into the ocean doing cartwheels.

"Hey! What are you doing!?" Miina yelled from where she sat in the shallow water. Karen had swallowed some sea water and half-cried, "Waah, that's salty!"

"Hahahaha! Isn't this fun!?" Haruko celebrated her victory, paying no mind to Karen and Miina.

Watching the three of them play around like puppies, Maiku sighed where he stood, a ways off. "...Kids."

"They look like they're having fun. Let them be." Kosei took Maiku's hand. Some bizarre fashion sense had prompted him to wear purple bikini shorts. "Let's return to our mother, the sea, to a place where the senses have cast off the yoke of logic!"

Maiku shook off Kosei's damp hand and said, "You go by yourself!"

"You're always so cold! I thought you'd be more open with me if we came here!"

"There's a difference between being open and being a pervert!"

"Maiku, are you afraid? Don't worry, it only hurts at first. After that it feels real nice."

"What are you talking about!?"

Matagu, wearing a pair of knee-length swim trunks, eyed the two boys, who never seemed to be on the same wavelength.

"Oh. So you guys are like that."

Without even pausing long enough to blink, Kosei and Maiku responded.

"That's right."

"We are not!"

Maiku had clenched one hand into a fist and was trying to decide whether or not to punch Kosei, when he heard Tubaki's voice call from behind him.

"Kamishiro, would you help me put suntan lotion on?"

Maiku turned in the direction of the voice and saw her sitting with her legs folded under her on the vinyl sheet. She waved the bottle of suntan oil at him. She wore a black bikini with a very risqué design, as if she wanted to show off her nice body, much of it still pale inside the tan lines from her school swimsuit. The contrast made it very obvious that these were the parts of her body that were covered at any other time. It also put a lot of emphasis on just how much was exposed by the bikini.

"Me?"

While her breasts, easily too large to fit in a person's hand, competed to form deeper cleavage, Tubaki looked with some shock, trying to figure out what Maiku was thinking.

"Don't you want to?"

"Uh, no. That's not it."

"Then come help me."

She passed him the bottle and undid the strap of her bikini. Then, holding the bikini on with one arm, she lay face-down on the sheet.

When she did, the soft swells of her chest spread out into round pillows on both sides. The bikini bottom stretched tight across her like a second skin, plainly showing a smooth form. Flustered by Tubaki's sensual body, which was almost a traitor to her intelligent features that looked so good in her frameless glasses, Maiku opened the lid of the suntan oil. He then noticed that Kosei, who he hadn't seen leaving, was suddenly missing. Maiku looked around to see where he had gone, and saw him walking angrily to the water's edge. He was usually a lot harder to get rid of, but this time he had gone, just like that. It was fine, but he felt strangely like something was missing. He squeezed a bit of the oil into his hand and started rubbing it into Tubaki's back.

"Mmm," Tubaki moaned as Maiku massaged her back with his oil-coated hands.

"Don't make weird noises."

"Sorry. I'm a little bit ticklish."

Matagu looked like he was about to drool as he watched the oil soak into Tubaki's white back -- such a contrast to her tanned arms and legs.

"Hey, Ichigo," he said.

"No."

"I haven't even asked you anything!"

"Sorry, I don't like being massaged by someone with an ulterior motive."

Matagu, who was planning on using the excuse of putting on suntan oil to do just that, was inwardly startled. "'Ulterior motive?' What do you mean? I'm completely innocent."

"Really?"

29

"Of course."

"You're saying that if I pushed my swimsuit down to my waist to bare my back, and let you trail your oil-covered hands over my pale skin, and even if I became flushed or started breathing heavily, you would not entertain any ulterior motives?"

"O-of course not!" Matagu's voice broke a bit, imagining the scene Ichigo had described in her flat voice.

"And after you finished rubbing oil on my back, I bet you'd believe I would say 'Now let me do you' and you lay on your back', and after I coated the front of your curve-less body with oil, I'd straddle you, and our skin would be pressed together. I'd twist my nubile body around on top of you, pressing my soft breasts up to you. With the deceiving curve of my crotch, still covered only in the dark blue fabric of my old school swimsuit, I'd test how hard the small bulge in the front of your swim trunks had become, and say, 'Oh my, it's already this hard.' And even if I did all that, you would still be completely without any ulterior motives or impure thoughts?" Ichigo said, staring intently at Matagu's face.

He wore a blank stare. He got up, but not fully. He was still partially bent over.

"I have to go to the bathroom."

"Number one or number two?"

Perhaps because it was neither, Matagu hurried away without answering her question.

"He's so young," Ichigo murmured watching him leave.

"Wow! There's an outdoor hot spring!" Miina said, impressed as she stepped from the changing room into the ladies bath. She was naked, but held a towel in one hand. The rest of the group had gathered on the rocks that surrounded the spring. She watched the steam float up from the hot spring, spreading into the fast-approaching summer night.

"This is my first time in an outdoor hot spring!" Karen added, impressed. She held a towel lengthwise in front of her flat body.

"Mine too."

For Miina and Karen, who liked to spend as much time as possible soaking in the bath at home, this outdoor hot spring, with its perfect mood, made their hearts flutter. They had enjoyed their day at the beach to the fullest, playing beach volleyball, burying Matagu in sand, swimming races out to the off-shore buoys, piling more sand on the buried Matagu, eating the watermelon the man in the Hawaiian shirt brought them from the old lady at the inn, and watching the tide roll in to where Matagu was buried and unable to move. Their skin had burnt to a deep brown, and now the skin that was still pale looked very bright. It looked like they had been colored in black and white. While Miina and Karen stood in front of the hot spring, lost in their own admiration for it, Haruko raced out of the changing room, pushed through the space between where Miina and Karen stood and continued on to the hot spring.

"Last one in is a rotten egg!" Haruko jumped into the water wearing a pair of snorkel goggles on her head and carrying a rubber duck toy she liked. Water splashed everywhere.

"Hey! No fair!" Disappointed at being left behind, Miina jumped in right after her, and Karen followed. The three raced to get their naked bodies underwater, but the hot water stung on their sun burnt skin and they shrieked when it touched them.

"What's the racket?" Tubaki furrowed her brow at the voices echoing from outside the changing room, where she put the swimsuit she'd just taken off into a basket. Ichigo had undressed just a bit faster than Tubaki, with a towel in her right hand and a plastic water pistol in her left, made her way into the hot springs. Tubaki's eyes rested on the plastic gun, modeled after a Colt pistol, and asked, "What's that?"

"For self-defense."

"Huh?" Tubaki had a questioning look on her face, and Ichigo raised the gun to face-level and rested her finger on the trigger.

"It's filled with cumquat, kimchee mix, and bug spray."

Tubaki looked more and more confused, and when it got to the point that one could almost see the question marks floating around her head, they heard from the neighboring men's bath, "I wonder what that noise could be."

"Good question," Kosei responded politely from where he sat, soaking up to the shoulders in the spring. He moved closer to Maiku in the pool that was almost identical to the ladies' bath. "Maybe we should make some noise."

"What for?" Maiku moved around in the water to keep a distance between himself and the approaching Kosei. Here, his most important parts were unprotected and no action could be considered too cautious.

"It's depressing! Hearing them having all the fun"

"It doesn't sound like they're having that much fun."

Perhaps because he did not hear Maiku's comment, Kosei glanced at him meaningfully. "So we should do something fun."

"Do it by yourself, then."

"I don't wanna do it by myself in front of you." Whatever he was thinking of made Kosei's cheeks turn red. "Maiku, I didn't know you liked that sort of thing."

"Uh..."

Just when Maiku was gripped by an impulse to hold him underwater for fifteen minutes, this very unpleasant soul, the sliding door to the hot spring opened and Matagu walked in, his entire body covered in sand. He had somehow dug his way out of the small mountain of sand that had been piled on top of him by command of the student president.

Matagu washed the sand off his body using a bucket filled with warm water.

"Jeez, that was a pretty harsh prank."

Maiku felt, for his part, that Ichigo seemed to possess a kind of quiet vengeance she would express "when the time comes..." but Matagu had not picked up on that in the least, it seemed.

"Phew," Matagu sighed, climbing into the slightly salty water of the hot spring, looking up at the sky, its colors ranging from a clear orange to deep purple. The earlier excitement had not gone from the neighboring ladies' bath, and they could hear lively chatting voices.

"Whoa, Ms. Vice-President, you've got huge breasts!"

Matagu's eyes popped open the second Haruko's loud words flew over the wall.

"They're not that big." This was Ichigo. In her voice, they could almost hear her nose wiggling, contrary to her words.

"May I touch them?"

"What??" Tubaki responded with shock to Haruko's bold, but innocent request. Without waiting for a response, Haruko reached out to grab at the breasts where they floated in the water.

"Squeeze!"

"Ah, hey! Don't!"

"Tee-hee! Awesome! They really are big. They're too big to hold in my hands. And they're really soft and squishy!"

Matagu stood up in the water as if he could not bear it any more. With an incredibly serious look on his face, he pressed his ear up to the wooden fence that separated them from the ladies' bath.

"What are you doing?" Maiku asked, suggesting in the tone of his voice that what he did was a most reproachable act. Matagu turned toward him with an embarrassed look.

"Uh, well, it sounds like things are getting really weird over there."

You're the one getting really weird, Maiku thought.

"I don't think so."

"No, it's weird. It's definitely weird." Matagu nodded. "I think we should see what's going on."

"You mean you want to peep? In the ladies' bath?"

"Of course not! I can't believe you'd think that!" Having had his plans discovered, Matagu began acting in a plainly agitated manner. "It's just, you see, that outdoor hot springs are actually pretty dangerous. You could slip on a wet spot and fall and hit your head, or you could drown in the water or...."

"I don't think anyone's ever drowned in a hot spring," Maiku said, and Matagu became strangely determined.

"You'd think that, wouldn't you? People can drown in a shallow tub of water! You can't be too careful."

Maiku did seem to remember reading something like that in the notes in the margin of a comic magazine, but to tell the truth, he didn't think it was really connected.

"Then what do you mean, you want to 'see what's going on'? You're not going to climb the fence are you?"

Obviously, the fence was much higher than a person and there were no hand or footholds.

"Heh." Matagu's laugh seemed inappropriate for the situation. "Your concerns are unnecessary."

Maiku was extremely worried about where this was headed.

"I've been coming here since I was a kid. I know every inch of this hot spring." Matagu pressed his face close to the fence and began running his hand over the surface as if he was searching for something.

"There it is." Matagu had found a gnarl in the wood at a height that would be about eye-level for an elementary school student. He smiled complacently. "Just like always."

Matagu had somehow used a peep-hole from before to regularly peep in on the ladies' hot spring. Pulling at the gnarl that had been hollowed out by fingers, he stooped down and pressed one eye up to the hole.

"Hey!" Maiku, who had been watching this and did not really think he would be able to see into the ladies' bath, became flustered and stood up in the water. Behind that fence was not only Tubaki and Ichigo, but Miina and Karen were there too, completely exposed in the water. He couldn't just sit by and watch as Matagu committed this shameless act. However, just as he was raising his arm to grab his wicked upperclassman's shoulder, Matagu gave a terrible scream.

"Aaaaaaaaahhhhh!" Matagu fell head first into the water with a huge splash.

"What was that scream?" Miina, who had been sitting comfortably with her back against the rim of the pool, sat up straight and stared over at the fence. Karen and Haruko looked in the same direction, wide-eyed. Meanwhile, Tubaki noticed Ichigo was standing ready near the fence, water pistol in hand.

"Ms. President, what was that?"

Ichigo lowered the pistol she had just fired through the gnarl in the fence. A small smile appeared on her face.

"The bug spray."

"Well, what's next?" Matagu, one eye red and swollen, looked around at everyone's faces where they sat in a circle, as he shuffled the cards. Everyone was playing cards in the boys' room after finishing a dinner, the main course of which was more sashimi than they could eat. They all felt warm after sitting in the hot springs and now relaxed in yukata the inn had provided them. They had played poker, hearts, slap, and every card game they could think of. They were all beginning to get sick of cards and no one was responding to Matagu's question.

"I'm getting sick of playing cards," Ichigo said, speaking for them all, and Matagu stopped shuffling the deck.

"Should we play another game then?"

"Another game?" Miina asked, and Matagu replied immediately.

"Since we've got guys and girls here, how about we play the king game?"

To play the king game, you mix slips of paper with numbers

written on them. One of the pieces of paper has "king" written on it. The person who draws the "king" slip can give orders to all the rest. The king's orders must use the numbers, for example: "Numbers 1 and 5 must kiss" or "Number 3 must do a head stand." Because the numbers are face-down, the king won't know who has which number, leading to some unexpected results. This is what makes the game fun. Because it is played a lot at big parties to promote friendship between the guys and girls, the king's orders often include things like making people kiss or touch each others' chests. When Matagu suggested the king game, a huge range of thoughts crossed Miina, Karen, and Tubaki's minds.

With a bit of luck, they might be paired with a certain someone and get to kiss him or do this and that with him.

But while everyone else was considering the possibilities, Haruko protested.

"The king game? I hate that game!"

"What? Why?" Ichigo asked.

"Sometimes I play that game just with my brother. I always end up being kissed or touched or made to wear glasses or all sorts of other weird things."

The idea of the king game is that no one knows who will have to carry out the king's orders, so a game only involving "the king and one subject" would have no point. It was clear as glass that this was a dirty plan of Matagu's to take advantage of Haruko's innocence and increase bodily contact between them. Matagu, who had done things to his sister that could only be called domestic sexual harassment, now was met with gazes of contempt and hatred by everyone else in the circle.

"What? Aren't you interested in playing the king game?"

Matagu looked very uncomfortable and, seeming unable to endure everyone's piercing stares, suggested another game. "It is a summer night, perfect for giving dares to test our courage."

Tests of courage...

Reflexively, Miina imagined herself screaming and clutching at Maiku. This might be a good chance.... She clapped her hands together and said, "That sounds great!"

"It is not great! I hate being scared." Karen said in a pitiful voice, her eyes filling with tears just from hearing the words 'tests of courage.' Miina put her arm around Karen's shoulder, turning her away from the group and whispered something in her ear. She may have told her she could have a chance to be alone with Maiku during a dare.

"Well, I guess I'm for the tests of courage." Now that she'd come around from her previous opinion, Karen spoke eagerly.

Tubaki's eyes shone brightly behind her glasses and she said, "I'll do it, but how about you, Kamishiro?"

"I guess I'll play," Maiku said, not looking too eager about it, and Kosei, sitting next to him, also nodded his approval of the game.

Seeing there was no particular reflexive opinion, Matagu spoke in disturbingly high spirits, "Tests of courage it is then!"

Ichigo looked coldly at the strangely excited Matagu and spoke in a voice so low only he could hear. "You never learn, do you?"

Matagu's face twitched, but he pretended not to have heard.

"A little ways down the road is a small shrine. How about if we break into pairs of one girl and one guy and walk there and back in turns?"

"Pairs of one guy and one girl? That sounds good!" Miina made a fist, and Karen nodded, "That's a great idea."

"But don't we have two girls too many?" Tubaki asked coolly.

"The extra girls can try to scare everyone else."

"But who will they be?"

"Well... I guess the two oldest should..." Miina said, and Tubaki's right eyebrow shot up.

"Why? Shouldn't the younger ones have to yield to us?"

"That's bossy. I think it's unfair to distinguish by class," Karen complained, squaring her shoulders.

"Then let's draw straws," Matagu said, going over to his bag and preparing strips of paper with a very practiced hand. He came back in a bit with thin strips of paper, three in one hand and five in the other.

"These are for the guys," he said, holding his right fist out to Kosei. To Miina and the other girls, he held out his left fist and said, "And these are for the girls."

Miina and Karen hesitated, unsure whether or not to accept the idea of drawing straws, but Haruko went right ahead and took one. Tubaki and Ichigo went next, and Miina and Karen reluctantly followed their example.

After Maiku and Kosei had picked, Matagu kept the last strip for himself and asked, "What number did everyone get? Whoever has the same numbers are a pair."

There were different numbers written at the bottom of each strip of paper.

"I'm three," Haruko said.

"We're a pair then," Kosei responded.

Then Tubaki spoke, "I'm two."

"Then we're together," Maiku said, destroying Miina and Karen's hopes.

That meant....

Miina looked up timidly from her paper with the number one written on it. The only boys here were Maiku, Kosei, and Matagu. Maiku was paired with Tubaki, and Kosei with Haruko, so Miina's partner had to be the one remaining.

"I'm number one..."

"You're with me."

When she looked at Matagu, who was trying to smile coolly, she felt as if she had just dived into a bathtub full of caterpillars.

This could not be any worse.

"That means we'll be scaring everyone," Ichigo said, showing Karen her paper with an "X" written on it.

"Yeah, what a shame."

"Everyone has their partners, so let's get started," Matagu said and started to get up, but Ichigo spoke in a dark, gloomy voice.

"This reminds me of another time I played this game." Everyone focused their attention on Ichigo and Matagu's body stiffened in surprise. "It was when I was in middle school..."

It seemed the story was on a different topic than the one Matagu had feared, and he calmed.

"I was on a trip for a school club, staying in an inn near the sea, like this one. There were eight of us, including our advisor. It was night and we'd all had supper and taken our baths, and we had too much time on our hands. At the suggestion of the club president, we decided to have a test of courage. She said she'd seen a small shrine on a cape between the beach and the inn. It wasn't far, so we decided we'd go there and come back one at a time. Our advisor liked that kind of thing, so she said she thought it sounded like fun and would do it, but there was one girl in the group who said we shouldn't. We'll just call her 'A.' 'A' was actually related to the owners of the inn and the reason we had chosen that inn to stay at was because we could get a good deal through her connection. 'A' was a quiet, but level-headed girl, and you could say she was strong-minded. She wasn't the type to be afraid of a little test of courage. When we asked her why she was against it, she wouldn't say at first.

"Finally, she told us this: A long time ago, at the beginning of the Showa Period (around 1926), a life raft was cast ashore one day. There were seven people on board and they all looked exhausted. They were survivors of an accident at sea that had sunken a ship several days before. All of them had crowded onto the small life raft and had somehow managed to drift ashore there. Despite narrowly avoiding death, they all wore dark expressions. At first everyone thought it was because they were so tired, but even after they were admitted to a local hospital and their strength gradually returned, no sign of happiness returned to their faces. Eventually, one of them confessed the following, perhaps because he could no longer bear his guilty conscience.

"He said they were murderers. After the ship had sunk, there had been eight of them on the life raft. Well, to be accurate, eight of them had tried to get in the life raft, but the capacity of the life raft was five and no matter how hard they tried, they couldn't fit more than two extra people on board. If one more had tried to climb on, the raft would sink. One of them would have to be sacrificed in order to save the rest. At that time, there were demons in the hearts of everyone on board the raft. Among those on the life raft was a poorly-dressed old man. When the accident had occurred on the ship, he had received injuries to his chest. He had lost a lot of blood and didn't seem like he'd be able to make it until help arrived. The other passengers decided this, climbed onto the life raft and pushed the old man into the sea when he tried to climb on after them. He was old and didn't have much longer to live, plus he was injured. The seven told themselves they had to do this to survive and pushed his hand away when he grabbed desperately for the boat, and then finally pushed his injured body into the sea with the oar. Even so, the old man wanted to be saved and struggled to get near the boat as it floated between the waves. When he did, they used the oar to push his nearly-bald head underwater. The man sunk beneath the water's surface many times, until finally he never rose again..."

Everyone listened seriously to this ghastly story, which Ichigo told them in an emotionless voice.

"In the end, that story went public, there was a trial, and the seven survivors all received suitable societal sanctions. And they put together some money and built a small shrine on the cape that overlooked the sea where the ship sank to appease the spirit of the old man they had driven to death. But in the end, it didn't work out so well. Naturally.

Even though they'd committed a crime, the seven had survived. On the other hand, the old man, whose life had been taken so cruelly, would never live again. The reason the seven built the shrine was not because they truly regretted having committed their crime, but to escape their own guilty consciences. This selfish 'atonement' would not appease the old man's spirit, and soon after the shrine was built, there were many reports of monstrous phenomena. Nothing happened during the day, but if you went to the shrine after sunset, they say you'd hear a voice whispering 'One too many, one too many,' even though there was no one around. Those who lived near the shrine started saying the ghost of the one man who didn't get on the life raft wandered around at night. The villagers were afraid and had the shrine exorcised many times, but nothing helped. They say you can still hear the ghost of the old man's voice if you go near the shrine at night."

As Ichigo's story continued, Miina and Karen kept moving closer and closer to each other and were gripping each other's hands tightly.

"So that's why 'A' said the test of courage was a bad idea. But we were sitting out in the middle of nowhere, bored to death, with no TV and no video games. Her story had the opposite effect on us. If there really were monstrous phenomena, we wanted to see them. Everyone thought it sounded like fun and got even more interested in the game. I'd be lying if I said I didn't think her story was creepy, but even if something did happen, we'd just hear the ghost's voice, and be a little scared. I think everyone was thinking along those same lines. So, we ended up over-ruling 'A's refusal, and went ahead with the test of courage. Then Kiri..."

Ichigo looked flustered when she almost said the girl's name, after using a pseudonym up until that point. She continued.

"No, 'A' stubbornly refused to join in. Finally we had no choice but to leave 'A' in the room and go ahead with the test of courage, just the seven of us. A narrow path stretched from the inn to the cape. Our advisor went first along that path, carrying a pocket flashlight. It must have taken her about fifteen minutes to go and come back. When she came back, she had a strangely scared look on her face and she said she had heard a hoarse voice near the shrine saying 'One too many, one too many' even though there was no one else around. At first, I thought she must have made it up to make the test of courage more interesting. That teacher who was our advisor liked pranks and would sometimes baffle half the class with unrelated small-talk. But, the next girl who went, and the next, both said they'd heard the same voice saying 'One too many' when they came back. And the next and the next after that were the same. Finally, all six girls who had gone before me came back with the same story, and then my turn came. The teacher gave me her flashlight and said it was all right to quit if I was afraid, but I decided to go. I didn't want them to think I was chicken and I also wanted to hear the creepy voice they all described. Plus, all six who had heard the voice came back unharmed, so I figured I'd just be a little scared, but nothing else would happen to me. The six of them saw me off, with worried faces, and I walked down the narrow path, using the flashlight to light the way. It was a moonless night, and so dark I couldn't see my hand in front of my face. I walked wearily down the path, guided only by the light of the flashlight. I'd be lying if I said I wasn't discouraged. Before long, I reached the cape and saw the shrine near its point. I approached it fearfully, listening carefully all around me..."

Ichigo paused for emphasis and Karen, who looked terrified, and should have been too scared to ask, asked, "Wh-what happened next?" though she looked like she wished she could have stopped herself.

"Nothing happened. I didn't hear anything."

Karen relaxed her death-grip on Miina's hand.

"Of course, I heard the waves from the ocean, but that was all. No matter how long I waited, I didn't hear any creepy voice. I thought I might be in the wrong place, so I walked all around the shrine. Then I thought it might be the light, so I turned off my flashlight, but even then there was no voice. I lost track of the time, and when I went back I found out they'd been worried because I took so much longer than anyone else. They asked me if anything had happened. I said I hadn't heard any strange voice and asked them if they all really had. At that, everyone became uncertain. They said they thought they had heard something, but it was drowned out by the waves. Then I thought they must have all fallen for our teacher's trick. They'd heard that scary story, then the first person to come back from the shrine says she heard a voice, and everyone after her hears the voice too... it was just a mental state. Because of that, they must have mistaken the sounds of the waves and the leaves rustling for a voice. Just when I started to believe this, I felt a chill come over me and we all went back into the inn. When we got back to the room, 'A', who should have been waiting for us was..."

Ichigo paused to let her words sink in and continued after a superb pause.

"Dead."

Karen drew in a sharp breath. Her hand, still clasped in Miina's, was clammy with sweat.

"'A' was lying face-down in the middle of the room. Her forehead looked like it had been hit repeatedly with a blunt object and a lot of blood had pooled out around her. It was so horrible we couldn't even speak, but just kept standing there looking down at her dreadful corpse. Then, suddenly, we heard a hoarse voice from behind us and it sounded like it said this..."

Someone swallowed and it sounded too loud.

"Now there are seven."

Ichigo finished her story and closed her mouth. The center of the room was absolutely quiet. For a while, no one said anything.

"Well, about time we got going." Ichigo broke the heavy silence and stood up as if nothing had happened.

"Th-that's right," Matagu got up next.

"Oh, hold on a minute. I'll get a flashlight ready."

"Well then, I'll get ready to scare you," Ichigo said, going to the next room and rummaging through her things.

"M-m-m-m-m-miina?" Karen's voice quavered like a cicada's and she grabbed at the sleeve of Miina's yukata.

"What?"

"W-w-will we be all right on the test of courage?"

"Huh? What are you talking about? Of course we will."

"B-but in the story..."

"Come on, it's just a story. Don't be so scared."

Even though her body had been rigid while Ichigo told the story, compared to the quivering Karen beside her, Miina looked very composed.

"But it's just like in the story. There's the ocean, an inn, a test of courage, and there are eight of us all together. Eight people! As in 'one too many'!"

"What about it?"

"So, if there's one too many..."

"Calm down. Even if Ms. President's story is true, it was a different place. It has nothing to do with us."

"Oh... That's right. It has absolutely nothing to do with us, has it?"

"Umm..." Miina paused. "Of course not."

"Why did you pause? There is some connection, isn't there? Isn't there!?"

While Miina teased Karen, Matagu came back with the emergency flashlights he had gathered without permission hugged close to his chest. Ichigo seemed ready, and came out of the next room carrying the vinyl tote bag she'd brought to the beach. When they were all ready, they streamed out of the inn. They walked on the small road to the forest behind the inn, relying on the light of one flashlight per pair. Matagu was in the lead. Eventually, the road forked. One branch continued straight forward, and the other veered away at a slight incline. Matagu stopped and pointed his flashlight down the hilled path.

"The shrine's that way," he said.

The narrow road led through a grove and ran into the darkness parallel to the slope of the mountain.

"It should take about fifteen minutes to the shrine. It's the only path, so you won't get lost."

Matagu reached into the breast of his yukata and pulled out some of the paper he used when they drew straws.

"I'm going to go first and leave this paper in the shrine. Each pair that goes after will have to pick up the paper with their number written on it and bring it back. Got it?"

That meant that if everyone had to bring back a piece of paper from the shrine, no one could chicken out in the middle because the paper would be proof that they made it all the way.

"We'll go ahead so we can get ready to scare you." Ichigo held a penlight she'd brought herself. She turned toward Karen and said, "Come on, you too."

"Y-yes." Karen started after Ichigo, but Miina pulled on the sleeve of her yukata and stopped her. Miina led Karen away from the group.

"Karen, the fourth code of the Love Alliance."

"Huh?"

The fourth code was "If any other girls try to approach Maiku, we will work together so they cannot get close to him." Miina nodded toward Tubaki.

"Do everything you can to get in their way so the hoochie girl with glasses doesn't get too cozy with Maiku. Got it?"

"Yes. I'll do all I can."

Now that the Love Alliance had been brought into it, Karen, who had up until now been frightened, narrowed her eyes. Her fear had thinned some now that she had the goal of cutting off someone who got in the way of their love.

"What are you doing? Let's hurry."

"Oh, sorry."

When Ichigo called her, Karen followed in the geta sandals from the inn, they sounded two or three steps on the hard pavement before stepping onto the path. The path was dark on that moonless night and the light that shone from the emergency flashlight on the path in front of her was her only help. The darkness of the late night that surrounded her was dense in a way she could never have imagined in a city where there was always some artificial source of light. It made her think it would not be surprising to hear there were beings from a different world wandering around in that darkness.

It was too bad she was not paired with Maiku, but in a way, she was relieved her role was just to scare people on the test of courage. It was scary just to be walking around in this darkness, but if she had to deal with people trying to scare her too, she would definitely scream and start crying. Depending on the circumstances, she might even wet herself. But because she was the one who would be scaring other people, at least they wouldn't be scaring her, and for someone who frightened as easily as she did, that was something to be thankful for.

"About here looks good." When they'd walked just ten minutes, Ichigo went off to the left of the path and pushed her way into the grove. Karen was feeling nervous because it was the sort of place where it seemed strange hands would grab your arm if you misstep, and pull you off into some place you'd never be able to get out of. Ichigo held her pen-light below her face and said, "Hurry up."

Even though the light cast frightening shadows over Ichigo's face, Karen stepped over the grass to her side. When she came into the grove, Ichigo broke a meter-long branch from a nearby tree and then plucked off all the leaves and twigs, leaving one straight stick. She then reached into her tote bag and pulled out some string from her sewing kit. She tied this to one end of the stick, and to the dangling end of string, she tied a hook she'd made from a hairpin. Karen watched her, wondering what she was doing, and Ichigo pulled some konnyaku from her tote bag and hung it on the hook.

"Done." Ichigo passed the stick with the konnyaku dangling from it to Karen. "You know how to use this, don't you?"

"Yes. More or less." Hiding in shadows, you'd dangle the konnyaku on people's necks as they walked by. It was a trick they often used in haunted houses in school festivals. "By the way, why'd you bring kon-nyaku?" Karen couldn't imagine she'd brought the gelatinous tuber cake along as a snack to eat in the car.

"I actually had intended to use it in the secret retreat, but it came in handy for this too."

What kind of secret retreat would need konnyaku?

She wanted to know what they would use it for, but she felt she probably shouldn't ask and let the topic go at that.

"I have to get ready too." She then pulled from her bag a head-band with cat ears attached to it, and a collar with a large bell. Karen could only imagine they were for the secret retreat too. Ichigo put them on with a practiced hand.

"What are those?" She asked, and Ichigo held a fist lightly up to her chest, and made a motion of beckoning something.

"Can't you tell? It's a ghost cat."

I think it's a bit off...

As if shutting out any further questions, Ichigo turned her back on Karen's questioning face.

"I'm going to go a bit farther ahead, so you stay here. Good luck." After the yukata-wearing, self-proclaimed ghost cat left, Karen suddenly felt helpless all alone in the grove. She looked out between the trees they'd entered through, and stretched her neck out to wait for the first pair to come. She finally saw the glow of a flashlight in the distance.

Here they come...

Karen switched off her own flashlight and breathed quietly in the grove. The first pair to come was Miina and Matagu, who had picked the papers with the number one written on them.

Aw, why does it have to be them...?

Matagu was holding the flashlight and Miina was walking at a short distance from him. In her head, she continued repeating the complaints she had annoyed everyone with earlier.

I wouldn't have done the test of courage if I'd known it'd be like this.

It sounded slightly selfish to be thinking this just because things had not gone as she had hoped, but it was not a surprising reaction to being paired with Matagu. Whether or not Matagu knew what Miina was thinking, he said nonchalantly, "It's dangerous for us to walk so far away. You should walk near me."

"I'm fine." Miina's reply was curt. She knew his intentions because she had been thinking of a similar idea. She walked quietly along, thinking something that would make Matagu cry to hear: That no matter how scared she got, if she wanted to hold on to Matagu, it would be better to hold on to a ghost. Before long, the pair, if they could be called that with the space between them, passed in front of the place where Karen hid in the grove.

Oof! Karen said in her mind, and flung out the branch with the konnyaku attached to it. The konnyaku swung like a pendulum toward Miina. But her timing must have been slow, because the konnyaku missed its target and whizzed through empty air behind her as she passed. 'Crap!' she thought, but it was too late. She could hardly run after them and drop konnyaku down their backs. Karen stilled her breathing and watched them walk away from her.

Awww, I messed up!

No one would be mad that she made a mistake, but it stung just the same. But, it didn't really matter. This one was just practice. Karen regained her spirits and decided to wait with the flashlight still off for her next victims. It would only be another ten minutes before Maiku and Tubaki came. A small light glowed in the darkness, and slowly approached Karen.

"It's weird how dark it is. Like something's gonna jump out at us. I'm scared." Contrary to her words, there was no hint of fear in her voice. Maiku was carrying the flashlight, but Tubaki took his free arm and hooked hers through it.

"Hey!" He said, flustered from having his arm pressed up to her ample chest. Tubaki did not seem to be wearing a bra and through the thin fabric of the yukata, he could feel elasticity beneath the softness.

"I don't feel safe unless I do this. It's all right, isn't it?"

Maiku could hardly ask her to let go after being told this. Maiku fumbled for words and Tubaki took the opportunity to squeeze the younger boy's arm closer to her. When she did, his arm caught the neck of her yukata, where some cleavage showed. Karen watched closely under the cover of night, and had not been able to see everything, but she knew the detested hoochie girl with glasses was initiating more bodily contact than was necessary.

There was no mistaking it; circumstances called for Love Alliance code four to be brought into play. She actually wanted to run out of her hiding spot and physically split them up. But being unable to bring herself to do that, first she would threaten Tubaki with the konnyaku attack.

Karen aimed for Tubaki's face and cast the stick, like one might do when fly fishing. Even though she was very careful this time to avoid mistakes, it seemed, though perhaps she imagined it, that her timing was a bit fast. The konnyaku flew past Maiku and Tubaki's faces and swung back at Karen, like a pendulum.

"Huh?" Maiku noticed something move in front of his eyes, and pointed his flashlight at the trees where Karen was hidden. With a bright light suddenly pointed at her, Karen reflexively shut her eyes. Then, the konnyaku whizzed past her ears, and came right back at her neck.

"Eeek!" Karen squealed, feeling something cold touch her neck. If she had stopped to think about it, she would have realized it was the konnyaku attached to the end of her own stick, but she had not had the time for that. Thinking a ghost had touched her neck, she threw down the stick she was holding, and ran out of the grove, with every hair on her body standing straight up.

"Aaah!" Maiku screamed, surprised by the black lump that flew out furiously from the circle of light cast by his flashlight. Running from something behind her that didn't exist, Karen dashed without looking toward Maiku. They collided, and Tubaki, who had let go of Maiku's arm in shock, fell over backwards. Maiku was unable to stop Karen's forceful run, and the two of them fell into the grove on the opposite side of the trail. Unfortunately, on that side of the path was a steep slope and Maiku and Karen tumbled helplessly down it.

"Wh-what the hell was that?" Tubaki said in a stutter, still sitting on the dirt road where she had fallen. The flashlight was still in Maiku's hand and she was in complete darkness. For the time being, she stood up, seeing nothing better to do.

"Kamishiro! What happened? Where are you?" Tubaki called out haphazardly into the darkness in an uncharacteristically worried and nervous-sounding voice. After a moment, a light hovered idly, and Maiku called out from behind the trees, "I'm down here, Tubaki!"

"Kamishiro!" Tubaki entered the grove and stopped before the slope, looking down at the light's source. The light showed the slope to be made of bare clay, and was steeper than she'd imagined. There were no visible hand or foot-holds and the slope looked impossible to climb.

"Are you all right? Are you hurt?"

"I'm fine. I just skinned my knee, nothing bad." Maiku's voice was steady and Tubaki rested her hand on her chest in relief.

"What was that before?"

"It's Karen."

"Onodera?" Tubaki was taken aback, but Maiku continued, "I don't think we can climb out of here, but could you go back to the inn and get some rope or something?"

"All right," Tubaki said, but then realized she had no light to find her way back. "I can't. I don't have a light. I'd never make it back to the inn like this."

"Then can you wait there in the middle of the road? The third group should come soon. Would you explain what happened and go back with them?"

"Sure. That seems like a good idea," Tubaki replied and stepped out of the grove.

Phew, that should work, Maiku thought and sighed, then pointed the flashlight at Karen.

"What were you doing?"

"Um, I'm supposed to scare you, so I thought I'd surprise both of you by... " Karen replied, fixing her yukata, which had become disheveled in the fall.

"Suddenly jumping out at us?"

"Not exactly..."

"Well, it doesn't matter." Maiku sat down at the foot of the slope and waved Karen to sit by him.

This is getting pretty serious.

Karen sat down next to Maiku, hugging her knees to her chest, half-burying her depressed-looking face in them. She had succeeded in scaring Tubaki out of her wits and separated her from Maiku, but she'd also landed herself in an awful situation. She couldn't see too well in the dark, but it seemed they'd fallen pretty far, and they had both been fortunate to not be seriously hurt.

I wonder if Maiku's mad at me.

Maiku shone the flashlight at the thicket in front of them, and she couldn't see his face in the darkness. While Karen was wondering whether she should apologize for all this or if saying something stupid would have the opposite effect, Maiku spoke, looking straight ahead.

"I'm glad you're all right." It was a bit gruff, but Karen found herself becoming nervous over these unexpected kind words.

"Um, yes. You too."

Good. He doesn't seem too mad.

Karen's spirits lifted, just from knowing that. She had put him in a bad mood many times, but then, Miina had always been with her. If they both messed something up together, he got mad at both of them together. It was like they were twins, bound by some unbreakable bond. So now, in a rare chance to be alone with Maiku, it was different, and she felt uncomfortable, for some reason. If she had made Maiku mad at a time like this, she would not have known what to do, and might have started to cry.

I'm really glad she hadn't made Maiku mad now that we're alone like this. If he'd been mad, I'm sure I would have....

As soon as she thought that, Karen became quite conscious of the fact that she and Maiku were alone together.

I'm alone with Maiku.

As soon as she realized this fact again, her heart lept inside her. Even though she was just sitting by him, hugging her legs, her heart raced and blood rushed to her cheeks.

What am I so excited for?

The place where they sat, side-by-side, was so quiet, it seemed every sound was swallowed by the darkness. They both sat silently in that silence, and Karen felt the beating of her heart must be audible to Maiku.

"Karen." Maiku called her name in the darkness, still facing forward. Even though he didn't say it very loudly, it echoed in Karen's ears.

"Um, about before..."

"Before?"

"Uhh... you know, when I.... uh... and you passed out."

"Huh?"

She passed out all the time, so unless he told her more details she wouldn't know which time it was.

"You know..." Maiku raised his voice in annoyance, but quickly lowered his voice. "That time we kissed, accidentally."

"Ah, oh... yes." That incident replayed in her mind. Karen was about to collapse in the dining room, when Maiku had caught her. But Maiku quickly lost his balance and their bodies had become entangled, falling on the floor. Then Maiku's lips touched Karen's by chance as he fell on top of her.

It had been a complete accident and they could not really say they had kissed, but their lips had touched.

"I still haven't apologized for it. I'm sorry."

Karen was flustered by these unexpected words.

"Oh, well, that's all right. You don't have to apologize. I don't think about it." That was a lie. Accident or no, Karen considered it her first kiss. She couldn't forget it easily. She could not remember the exact feel of having her lips touch his, but she had never forgotten for a second that she had kissed Maiku.

"Oh." There was a complex quality to the emotion in his voice in this response, but it was so short it was impossible to read. "You're not thinking about it anymore. That's good."

Karen started to speak, as if by reflex, but she felt like she was out on a limb and let his words sink in. She did not know exactly what she had been about to say, but she felt like it was something she would not be able to take back, once she said it.

The pair returned to silence. With her head still resting on her knees, Karen turned and stole a glance at Maiku through the darkness. But with his flashlight pointed in the wrong direction, all she could make out was the outline of his face, with no idea of its expression. Even though she was annoyed by that, she was also thankful they were in complete darkness. If they had been in the noon-time sun, Maiku would have seen how red her face was.

Karen began to feel suffocated by the idea of sitting next to Maiku in silence forever. She felt like she wanted to scream, or break out running for no reason. Squeezing her legs tighter than she needed to, she knew that although she could endure this inexplicable desire, she would soon boil over with another desire from within her body. At first, she thought the pressure in her lower abdomen was imagined as a result of feeling suffocated, but gradually, she realized it was real, and that she had to go to the bathroom.

I gotta pee...

It was summer, but because she was sitting directly on the damp ground, she began to feel cold. She thought someone might come for them soon, and tried to hold it, but gradually the call of nature became too strong to ignore. 'Why did this have to happen now...?' she thought, but this was not something she could overcome through her will. Finally, she couldn't stand it anymore.

"Um, Maiku?"

"What?"

"I have to go."

Even in the dark, she could tell he had been startled.

"What are you talking about?"

"I'm sorry. I can't hold it anymore. I have to go to the bathroom."

"Oh, that."

What else could she have been talking about, Karen wondered, giving Maiku an imploring look. "What should I do?"

"If you can't hold it, I guess you'll have to go over there."

"What? In front of you?"

"Of course not!" Maiku spat at Karen's unbelievable misunder-standing. "Not there..." Maiku said, pointing with his flashlight at a spot a bit farther away. "You should be able to go in there."

Karen looked over at the outdoor toilet in the spotlight. She wouldn't have to be embarrassed about Maiku seeing her in there.

"But the sound..."

"The sound?"

"Yes. That is... when I..."

"Oh, that sound." Maiku felt his blood rush to his cheeks when he figured out what she meant. "All right, I'll plug my ears."

"Well then..." Karen stood up and Maiku handed her the flashlight.

"Watch your step."

"Thanks."

Karen pointed the flashlight at the ground and entered the thicket. She turned around, saw Maiku was completely engulfed by the darkness, and set the flashlight by her feet. Paying attention to where Maiku should be, Karen pulled down her underpants, tucked up her sleeves, and squatted.

"Maiku!" she called, and heard his reply a bit away.

"What?"

"Could you plug your ears?"

"Yeah."

Good. Now he won't hear anything embarrassing, she thought. While Karen felt her previous interaction with Maiku weighing on her mind, she felt everything that had been pressuring her gush out.

Ah, bliss...

With the impending danger taken care of, Karen felt herself relax. However, having relieved herself, Karen realized just then, as she started to do something she always did at such times, that she had not brought any tissues with her.

Oh no...

It seemed stupid when she thought about it. She had been so worried about where she could go, she had completely forgotten about tissues. She always had a sample packet of tissues they handed out on the street in the pocket of her skirt, but now she was wearing a borrowed yukata from the inn. Maiku was wearing the same thing and probably also didn't have any tissues.

What should I do?

She couldn't wait like this, but she thought it would hurt to use the leaves from nearby bushes. She could take off her underpants and use them to wipe herself, but then she'd have to be panty-less until she got back to the inn. Straddling the puddle she'd made, Karen worried about what to do, until a sudden rustling noise came from in the thicket. She looked in its direction, shone the light at it and saw it reflect back at her.

"Aaahhh!" Karen screamed without checking what it was she saw, and ran out of the thicket. Had she not just emptied her tank, she would have spilled it from fear and surprise. With unimaginably quick movements for her, she reached Maiku, his eyes wide and questioning, at the foot of the slope.

"Wh-wh-what happened?"

With her face pressed into his chest, she pointed toward the thicket she had just been using, and said, "Th-th-th-there's s-s-s-something in there!"

"Something?" Maiku was taken aback by her panic, but promptly took her flashlight and turned toward the thicket. When he did, he heard the rustling of branches and saw a black furry animal the size of a dog standing in the circle of light. It seemed to be a raccoon-dog. It must have been his eyes that reflected back at her.

"Don't worry. It was a raccoon-dog," he said in a flat voice.

"Huh?" Karen lifted her head away from Maiku's chest. Then, she heard Tubaki's voice from the top of the slope.

"Kamishiro! I've come back to help you!"

Maiku raised his flashlight to show where they were. "Tubaki, we're over here!"

"Maiku, Karen, are you all right?" came Miina's voice. If they listened carefully, they could hear Haruko and Kosei's voices as well. She must have gone back to the inn with the next pair, Haruko and Kosei, and then met the first pair, Miina and Matagu coming back from the shrine.

"Maiku, I'm gonna lower the rope," Miina said leaning over the slope's edge and pointing her flashlight down. The light poured down over them and hurt their eyes. Miina dangled the rope down as Kosei passed it from behind her. Looking down the slope, Miina saw the two standing in the circle of white light and screamed in shock, "Aaah!"

"Ooh, so that's what it was," Miina said in a disappointed voice, on the dark road back to the inn. She walked next to Karen, whose face was red enough to be visible even in the dark. It was not unexpected, for she had been seen without her yukata exposing her still-sore bottom, hugging Maiku tightly. She was glad Miina was the only eyewitness, because otherwise, she would have had to tell that embarrassing story to everyone, and not just to her.

"But I was so surprised! You were hugging Maiku with your bottom showing! I wondered what happened!"

"Let's not talk about it anymore." Karen said in a barely-audible

voice. Just like Maiku, walking in front of them, Karen's yukata was covered in mud from her fall down the slope. She would have to take another bath when they got back to the inn. Miina walked at the end of the procession along the narrow path and said to Karen, looking to the side at her red and downcast face, "I suppose you weren't so caught up in the confusion that you did anything to go against code one of the Love Alliance?"

Code one was that, "Until we know for sure which of us is related by blood to Maiku, neither of us shall confess our love to him."

"O-of course not!" Karen was startled, though she had nothing to feel guilty about.

"Oh." Miina nodded, but her face looked faintly like she hadn't completely accepted this.

After a while more of that, the group reached the inn, filed into the entrance and up the stairs, when Tubaki looked around and asked, "Where's Ms. President?"

Looking like they'd just remembered her, the other members of the group looked around at each other.

Karen turned to Miina and Matagu, the first pair, and asked, "Um, did you see her dressed up like... a ghost cat... of sorts?"

Matagu and Miina shook their heads.

"Then..." Karen looked at Kosei and Haruko who also said they hadn't seen her.

"That means no one has seen her since she split up with Karen?" Maiku muttered, to confirm the truth, and Tubaki looked like she was trying to conceal her worries.

"She'll be fine. You know her; she's probably already come back to her room."

Thinking with a bit of sadness that might be true, the group went upstairs and opened the doors to their rooms. Maiku groped at the switch by the door. The seven of them all froze the instant the lights went on and they saw the room. Ichigo, still in her yukata, lay face-down on the floor in a pool of blood. Her eyes were wide open as if she'd seen something awful, and the blood was drained from her face. Her body did not even twitch and she did not seem to be breathing.

"She's not dead, is she?" Matagu gasped, and Karen added in a shaky voice, "It's just like in that story she told. About the "One too many."

"That's ridiculous," Tubaki scolded them, but Karen wore an expression of pure terror.

"But... but it's exactly the same! When the rest came back from their test of courage, they found the eighth had..."

Karen stopped herself there, but each of the seven was thinking the word, 'died.' They couldn't help it, and they all drew in their breath at the monstrous phenomenon. Ichigo, who they had thought was dead, slowly got up, and said in a low, but clear voice, "Now there are seven."

"Aaaaaaahhhhhhhhh!!!!!!!!!!" Maiku, Miina, Karen, Tubaki, Kosei, Haruko and Matagu all screamed. When they stopped, Ichigo, sitting on the floor, wiped away the fake blood (she had perhaps brought along for the secret retreat) that hung from her forehead. She looked blankly at the seven passed-out bodies lying around her and said, "I wonder if I over-did it."

Chapter 8: Not related, not in love

"Why do we all have to come out here and eat together?" Maiku pouted as he sat down on a bench near some bushes. As soon as lunch started, Miina and Karen had come from the class next door to drag him off into the courtyard. Miina sat down next to him and looked up at the clear blue sky.

"Oh come on. It's such a beautiful day, we should eat outside."

"Plus, lunch is twice as delicious when the three of us eat together!" said Karen, moving in to sit on Maiku's other side.

Jeez.

Maiku, realizing it was impossible to resist them once they had their minds set on something, sighed to himself and opened his lunch that was handmade by Miina. Karen and Miina happily unwrapped their own lunch boxes and opened the lids. The smells of cool rice, light fried food, and pickled vegetables mixed together into the familiar "lunch smell" that tickled the three growing kids' noses. As if that mouth-watering smell had been carried off in the air around them, a refreshing breeze that rustled the treetops of the copse trees blew through the courtyard surrounded by the U-shaped school building. It was an ideal day for eating outside.

Maiku devoured his lunch ravenously, trying to satisfy his hunger. Miina brought her chopsticks to her mouth, examining the food she had prepared. Karen let her chopsticks hover over her lunch, deciding what to eat next. The three of them, with their three different ways of eating, filled their stomachs with their lunches.

"You look pretty interested in them," said Ichigo from behind

Tubaki who was standing by the window in the student council room, holding curry-filled bread in one hand and looking out at Maiku and the girls eating in the courtyard. Tubaki turned around. Ichigo, sitting in the president desk in front of the school flag, had already downed half of her tightly packed lunch held in an enormous aluminum lunch box that looked large enough to hold a dictionary. To the average person, her small physique and enormous lunch might seem incongruous, but for Ichigo this was a normal meal. Where could all that food go in such a petite body? In the entire time Tubaki had been eating lunch with Ichigo, she had never even seen her leave a grain of rice.

"I'm not really interested…" Tubaki said looking away like a child who had been caught sneaking food.

"You must be jealous," said Ichigo, shooting an angry look at Tubaki. She must have hit the nail right on the head, because Tubaki quickly changed her expression. Her grasp on the curry-filled bread tightened and curry oozed from the whole she had bitten. But, Tubaki recomposed herself within a second and looked Ichigo right in the eyes defiantly.

"You are welcome to think that."

"You're serious about him, aren't you?" For a moment, a look of hesitation crossed Tubaki's face.

"Yes," Tubaki said nodding very firmly, as if to push back any indecision she might be feeling.

"Alright, I'll help you," said Ichigo after a pause to make sure Tubaki was not going to change her mind.

"A piano concert?" Maiku, who had been summoned to the student council room after school, asked Ichigo with a questioning look on his face.

"An alumnus went to music school and is now a pianist. His name is Seizo Nishi. He performs in Japan and abroad and I heard that recently he won an international competition. And, with the help of our principal, we got him to agree to a commemorative concert for us. Like, a triumphant return concert," responded Ichigo from the president's chair in her usual monotonous voice.

"But why do I have to be on the planning committee for this concert?" Maiku pursed his lips. After all, he had been suddenly called here and assigned an unexpected job.

"Kamishiro, I'm paying a lot for your data processing skills. So…"

"So…? That doesn't mean you just assign me big jobs. I've already got my hands full with my own work."

"Of course, I'm not asking you to do it for free. I'll pay you an appropriate sum."

"You're not going to offer me a date with you again, are you?"

"If that's what you want, that's fine."

"No, that's OK."

"Well, how about this much?" inquired Ichigo, pulling out a small calculator from who knows where with hands as deft as a magician's. She quickly punched in some numbers and showed it to Maiku. Maiku's long face quickly disappeared, and he bowed his head to Ichigo.

"I'll gladly do it."

After being dismissed from the student council room, Maiku went to the conference room as instructed by Ichigo. There he found the vice-president, Tubaki, waiting for him alone. "First Meeting of the Piano Concert Planning Committee" was written on the blackboard in precise writing very fitting of Tubaki.

"I've been waiting for you. Sit down," said Tubaki sitting at a long desk in front of the blackboard. She patted the seat next to her, beckoning Maiku. The conference room, which usually had desks arranged in a U-shape, was empty and the only seat was the one Tubaki was urging him to sit in. Maiku reluctantly sat down and looked uncomfortably around the conference room.

"The other members of the planning committee haven't come yet?"

"There are no other members."

"Huh?"

"The only members of the Piano Concert Planning Committee are you and me."

"What?" Maiku raised his right eyebrow in question. "Why are there only two planning committee members?"

"There are only so many capable people available to help." Immediately after those words had left Tubaki's lips, the sound of Haruko's shrill voice filled the room from outside the open window.

"Leave me alone, bro!"

Wondering what was going on, Maiku looked out the window down to the courtyard and saw Matagu running after Haruko, who was walking ahead with her shoulders back.

"Come on, Haruko! It'll only take a second. Just one picture!"

"No way! Why should I suck on a popsicle while wearing black rimmed glasses, and an old-fashioned school swimsuit?"

"You don't understand. That's to emphasize how cute you are."

Maiku looked away from the courtyard and turned his eyes back to Tubaki. "It seems like there are plenty of people available to help."

"I said capable people."

"You've got a point." Of all the people to walk past the window, those two were certainly two of the least capable. They made Tubaki's point painfully obvious.

"Now that you understand, shall we get started with our meeting?"

"All right."

"I thought it seemed funny. So this is what they're up to!" whispered Miina, who was hiding in the bushes in the courtyard, trying to peek into the conference room window. Karen, who was crouching down next to her, scrunched up her face.

"Miina, this is major."

Even though Maiku had told them to head home without him, they had followed him to the student council room, and when they heard he was going to the conference room, they had staked out their current peeping spot to keep an eye on him. They were too far away to hear anything, but they could see that Maiku and Tubaki were alone and discussing something. That much was obvious. This was definitely a situation which called for the invocation of the fourth love alliance code: "If any other girls try to approach Maiku, we will work together so they cannot get close to him."

"We cannot let things go on like this," stated Karen, and Miina nodded deeply.

"Yeah. Let's go bother them."

"You won't be bothering anyone." Karen and Miina were so surprised by this response right in their ears that they almost fell over. They turned around, making sure they were still hidden by the bushes, only to see Ichigo's face so close they could feel her breath.

"Ms. President…"

"When did you…?" Karen and Miina stared at Ichigo with wide eyes. Ichigo was crouching down in the bushes just like them.

"While you were otherwise engaged."

"What do you mean, 'you won't be bothering anyone'? What are you going to do?" Miina asked in a biting tone, but while still keeping her voice low.

"I'd like to ask the same of you. Why do you want to bother them?" Ichigo retorted without even flinching.

"Um, well…" Miina stuttered. Ichigo looked her right in the eyes.

"Is it because this falls under code four of the love alliance?" Miina and Karen were incredibly surprised by this.

"H-how do you know about that?" Miina stammered. Ichigo, however, replied in her usual calm tone.

"Secrets never stay secret forever."

That may be true, but how could Ichigo know about Miina and Karen's secret love alliance? It was hard to believe. However, this was the student council president, sometimes known as "The Mossad of Kizaki High School." It was possible that she had found out.

"A love alliance… that might work well for you guys, but have you ever thought about what Kamishiro thinks?" said Ichigo to the two dumbstruck girls.

"What do you mean?" Miina asked, trying to regain her composure.

"Exactly what I said." Ichigo responded shortly. "If you try to get in their way, I'll do the worst thing possible."

"Wh… what's the worst thing possible?" asked Karen, hesitantly.

"Students at our school aren't allowed to have jobs," Ichigo whispered under her breath, as if she were talking to herself.

Miina and Karen drew back. They were just barely getting by with Maiku's income and the little money they got from their part-time jobs. If school officials found out that they were breaking the rules and working… well, it was pretty much a matter of life and death! For them that was really the worst thing possible. Actually, it was Ichigo who had (through Maiku) gotten them their jobs at the Fuchikawa shop. It was truly horrible of her to threaten them unscrupulously with the jobs she had found them.

Miina and Karen just sat there speechless. Ichigo, seeing that she had won, stepped out of the shadows of the bushes. Despite her small stature, she looked terribly large to Miina and Karen, looking up at her from their crouched positions.

Karen sunk down into the bathtub and sighed, causing the steam that was rising in the bathroom to falter. Miina, who was washing herself outside of the tub, stopped what she was doing.

"That's the 36th time."

"What?" Karen said looking at Miina blankly.

"The 36th sigh. You keep sighing!"

"You've been counting, Miina?"

"I can't help but count! Ever since we got home from school you've just been sighing."

Karen was even spacier than usual today and was not of any use at work. She was always pushing the wrong key on the register and slow to notice when customers called her, but on top of that, today when she was checking out a customer, she kept swiping Japanese stuffed-rolls over the scanner looking for a price tag that was not even there. She ended up rolling the rolls all over the scanner. It was so bad that the manager asked her if something had happened.

"Is what Ms. President said bothering you?"

"Yes," said Karen sitting stiffly in the bathtub. Miina had hit the nail right on the head.

"How does Maiku feel, I wonder...?"

"I wonder if our love alliance is annoying to Maiku."

"I guess maybe it is."

"Yeah…" Karen hung her head disappointedly and looked down at the bath water. She looked as if she would sink all the way into the tub if she stayed that way for too long.

"Since we can't tell Maiku our feelings right now because of… certain circumstances… we're trying to keep him from getting involved with any other girls. That's really selfish of us, isn't it?"

"Yeah, I guess it is," Karen expressed her agreement in a very weak voice.

"I know it is. It's self-centered of us. I know it's selfish." Miina's voice was shaking a bit, as if she were trying desperately to hold back her feelings that grew stronger and stronger. "But, can you give up just because it's selfish? I can't. I won't! I just… I won't give up on these feelings!" Miina squeezed the sponge she was holding and bubbles of body wash foamed up out of it.

"I won't either," said Karen, her head still hanging. "I've given up on so many things. Having a mom to come to parents' night, a dad to run with me in the school relay, grandparents to buy me Christmas presents, a family to eat dinner with, and…" As Karen listed off everything she had missed out on, it became more difficult to talk about all those things she had worked so hard to forget. As she got to the end of her list her voice was so faint one could barely catch what she was saying.

Karen…

It seemed like Karen was crying. While Miina was deciding whether or not to say something, Karen, who had been staring at her hands, resolutely lifted her head.

"I… I definitely won't give up either!" Her eyes were dry as she looked at Miina.

"That's more like it!" Miina smiled and added, "If my love alliance partner got depressed on me, I might get down, too!"

"I'm sorry."

"Oh yeah!" Miina said, as if remembering something. She stuck out her right pinky finger and put her arm out toward Karen. "Let's pinky swear."

"Pinky swear?"

"Yeah, that we promise not to lose hope, get depressed, or give up."

"Oh." Miina, realizing that Karen was not quite getting her

point, did her best impersonation of Mizuho Kazami.

"In this area, don't you pinky swear when you're making a big promise?"

Hearing this, Karen seemed to recall the odd conversation they had had when Maiku's homeroom teacher, Mizuho Kazami came to their house.

"Not just in this area, in the whole country!" said Karen laughing. She held out her right pinky. The two girls grasped pinkies and said in union, "Cross my heart and hope to die, stick a needle in my eye."

For the first time, Miina noticed a scar on the joint of Karen's right pinky.

"What?! The planning committee is meeting today, too?" exclaimed Miina, pouting. After school she had come to Maiku's classroom so they could all go home together, but he told her to go on ahead because of the meeting. Karen, who had tagged along, also looked unhappy.

"Does the planning committee really have to meet that often?"

"There aren't that many days left until the concert, so for a while we'll be meeting every day."

"No way!" Karen's reproachful voice rang through the hallway.

"Why don't you just say you can't go?" asked Miina.

"Yeah!" said Karen, nodding in agreement.

"I can't do that."

"Why not?"

"The pay is really good. We used up a lot of money on that vacation. I've got to make up for all that we spent."

Kosei had covered the round-trip train tickets and rooms, but they had gotten into the trip mood and bought a lot of snacks, ate out, and bought souvenirs. They spent a lot more than they had planned to.

"Is that really the only reason?" Miina looked at him with a doubtful look.

"What other reason could I possibly have?" said Maiku narrowing his eyes.

"You wouldn't possibly be infatuated with a certain woman... would you?"

"Of course not!" Maiku said, rejecting Miina's low-brow suspicions. But Miina was still not convinced.

"You seem awfully defensive. Very suspicious."

"Oh, give me a break."

"Even if you aren't interested in her, she is a hoochie girl with glasses. With a sexy body like that, I bet she's thinking dirty thoughts. You don't know what she might try when she's alone with you!"

"Ahem!" Miina and Karen turned quickly to look at who had cleared their throat behind them. It was Tubaki who had arrived to get Maiku with impeccably good timing.

"Who were you saying is thinking dirty thoughts?" she inquired, her glasses lens shining.

Miina was caught off guard for one second and before she could even open her mouth to respond, Maiku walked out of the room, practically pushing Miina and Karen out of the way.

"Thanks for coming to meet me, Tubaki."

"It's no problem," Tubaki smiled at Maiku, changing her expression from the one she had shown Miina and Karen. "It's already time for the meeting. We better get going, Kamishiro."

"Oh, yeah."

Tubaki walked off with Maiku wearing a huge smile on her face. Miina looked at them and stuck her tongue out.

"Well, Maiku's gone," lamented Karen. Miina put her hands on her hips and sighed deeply in response.

"Now I guess all we can do is hope that Maiku's apathy holds out," Miina said as she opened the front door and went inside. She and Karen had been talking about the situation the whole way home.

"Yeah," Karen said nodding flatly. She took off her shoes. Miina headed for the dining room still wearing her school uniform and holding her bag. She opened the refrigerator and took out a bottle of barley tea. She took out a glass, filled it with the cold tea and downed it. Karen handed her a glass and she filled it up with tea. Karen drank it in one gulp.

"I wonder if Maiku will be OK," she asked.

"I just wish there was someone who could watch them to make sure that hoochie girl with glasses doesn't try anything."

They would have stayed glued to Maiku's side after school to make sure certain upperclassmen with alluring bodies would not do anything inappropriate, but they worked almost every weekday afternoon so it was impossible to stay. It was not really something they could trust a classmate to do, so they just had to hope nothing happened. Miina had half given up as she rinsed her glass in the sink. Then, suddenly Karen yelled out.

"Oh!"

Miina was so surprised she practically dropped her wet glass.

"What are you yelling for? Don't surprise me like that!"

"Miina, I just thought of a great idea!"

"A great idea?"

"Yes, I thought of a person who could watch Maiku for us."

"Please don't say Haruko." Their classmate Haruko Shidou was the first person to come to Miina's mind because she seemed like the type who would help them just out of curiosity.

"No, really I shouldn't even say 'person' in this case."

"Huh?"

"Well, it's not necessarily a 'person.'"

"Are you talking about Haruko's brother?" Although at first glance he certainly seemed to be human, there was something different about Haruko's older brother, Matagu. Who else could Karen be talking about?

"Not him."

"Then who?!"

"Marie."

"What?!" Miina said, her eyes practically popping out of her head.

"Marie? You mean that little, round, sort of triangular girl?"

"Miina, that's Strawberry Milk you're thinking of."

"Oh yeah… sorry, you kind of surprised me."

Marie was a yellow creature, if you could call her that, small enough to fit in the palm of your hand, with a round face, and pointy head. Besides looking incredibly bizarre, she also had a floating red hoop around her waist, and the fact that she could fly made it hard to believe that she could possibly be from our planet. She loved sweets, particularly Puritti, a long stick like treat. Whenever Miina and Karen were having a snack she would appear out of nowhere like a stray cat and join them.

"But Karen, how can we ask Marie to watch Maiku?"

Considering that Marie was very small and could fly, she was the perfect candidate for stealthily observing Maiku. But would she really listen to their request? They were not even sure if she could understand their language. She could not possibly understand and carry out their instructions.

"I know how. Recently I've started communicating with Marie using gestures."

"Really?"

"Yes. Just leave it to me," Karen said, nodding with confidence. She took out a box of cookies from the bottom shelf of the cupboard. This was their snack box and it was filled with various half-eaten snacks. Karen opened the lid and brought out some Puritti. "Mariiiiie! I've got something for you! It's a yummy Puritti!" she called out waving the snack around in the air. After a while Marie appeared from out of nowhere and flew over to Karen.

"Noo!" responded Marie in a cheerful voice, clinging to the Puritti that Karen was holding. After gobbling it up in what seemed like an instant, Marie looked up at Karen with big round eyes that seemed to say, "Give me more!" Karen gave Marie another Puritti. After she finished that one, Karen offered her another snack. This continued until Marie had eaten much more than her own weight and looked very full. As Marie leaned back and rubbed her full stomach, Karen stood in front of her and began acting very strange. First, she brought her hands together in front of her chest and bowed to Marie. This seemed to be a gesture to let Marie know that she was making a request. Marie reacted to this and opened her narrow eyes wide. Karen's next gesture was incredibly puzzling to Miina. She first waved both of her hands by the side of her face and then suddenly made two fists, kneeled down on the floor on all fours, quickly stood up and spun around once. Then she seemed to be picking up something invisible and holding it under her arm.

Oh, so she's going to leave that aside for now.

Karen continued making incomprehensible gestures at Marie for what seemed like forever. Miina just stood and watched. Soon there was a bit of sweat visible on Karen's forehead and she seemed short of breath. Finally, Marie, who had been expressionlessly watching the strange actions of the Earth girl, suddenly stretched out her short arms and moved them about her body like a big ring. Apparently this was the gesture for OK.

"Thank goodness!" sighed Karen with relief. She turned to Miina with a huge smile on her face and said, "Marie says she'll do it!"

"Oh… is that what she said?" said Miina not knowing how else she could possibly respond to what she had seen. She smiled uneasily at Karen.

One week passed.

During that week Maiku had spent every day with Tubaki after school, working hard to plan the Piano concert. There were so many things to do: decide the set-up of the seats in the auditorium; prepare invitations for guests; order the flowers that a student representative would hand to the pianist after the concert. Maiku and Tubaki were looking over all the sheets keeping track of the money they had spent so far. In the back

corner of the conference room, Marie was watching them with wide eyes. Once she saw that the meeting was over, the strange yellow creature would go give a full report to Miina and Karen, who had just come home from their job. Of course, these reports were not given using language. She conveyed her reports from the low table in the living room using gestures that required the use of her entire body. Miina just watched these reports blankly, but Karen, who was a 'Ms. Enigma' herself, was able to understand. She watched with great interest, nodding and sometimes asking questions with her own bizarre gestures. When it was all over she would tell Miina, "Nothing happened."

You've got to admire her skill.

Everyday Miina felt more and more relieved that nothing was going on between Maiku and that hoochie girl with glasses. However, Maiku, who knew that Miina and Karen must be unhappy that he was spending every day with Tubaki, thought deep down that it was strange the two were not really complaining or getting in the way. Naturally it must have seemed strange to him that they would suddenly change their behavior. Little did he know they had a spy at his meetings and were receiving full accounts of everything that happened. Though, he would soon be paid and was so busy that he had little time to think about such trivial things. Meanwhile, the end of the piano concert preparations was in sight.

Tubaki looked over the sheet with carefully laid out the plans for the day of the concert on it.

"How does this look?" she asked, looking up at Maiku, who was sitting across from her.

"I think it looks good," Maiku nodded his approval. Tubaki set down the sheet she was holding and smiled sweetly.

"Wow, it looks like we're almost done then."

"Yeah," Maiku said, his expression softening at the thought of never having to spend his afternoons doing tedious work again. Tubaki noticed the look of relief and quickly changed her own expression to show her displeasure.

"You certainly seem happy about it, Kamishiro."

"Well, yeah, I guess so."

"Oh, I get it. I didn't realize how much you hated spending time with me," Tubaki said standing up and turning her back to Maiku. "I had no idea you hated me so much."

"No, no! That's not it at all," Maiku quickly tried to explain. Tubaki, with her hands behind her back, turned to Maiku, making her pleated skirt twirl. She bent down toward Maiku and looked him in the eyes.

"Then what is it?" Tubaki was so close, Maiku could feel her breath.

"Um..." Maiku looked down bashfully. His eyes happened to meet with Tubaki's cleavage, visible through her sailor uniform that opened in a V-shape, like the mouth of a milk carton.

Whoa!

Maiku blushed and looked away from the tantalizing fullness that was squeezed tightly by her uniform. Unfortunately, Tubaki noticed what Maiku had been staring at. She pulled her body away and covered her chest with her hands.

"Kamishiro, you pervert!"

"No, I... uh... didn't mean to..." Maiku mumbled incoherently.

Tubaki laughed.

"Geez, Kamishiro, you're bright red!"

"Don't make fun of me."

"Sorry," Tubaki said lowering her hands from her chest, taking a less defensive pose. "But, considering you live with two girls you seem very unfamiliar with such things."

"I hope you're not implying anything. There is nothing going on between us." Maiku turned away, frowning. Tubaki could not help but smile at his childishness.

Kamishiro is so cute. He almost reminds me of my bro...

When Tubaki realized what she was considering, her expression froze.

What was I thinking?

"Is there something wrong, Tubaki?" Maiku noticed Tubaki's stern expression and gave her a questioning look. Tubaki, as if she were trying to avoid meeting Maiku's eyes, suddenly turned around and walked out of the conference room. Despite almost running into a student walking past the room, she determinately walked down the hall without looking back.

"Wait... Tubaki!" Maiku hurried out the door and ran after Tubaki in a curt sprint, but someone grabbed his arm and stopped him abruptly in his tracks. Maiku spun around in annoyance, only to see Kosei staring at him with a steely look in his eyes. Tubaki had not noticed because she was in such a hurry, but she had almost run face first into Kosei.

"Shimazaki..." Maiku managed to gasp out his name, feeling confused and a little lost by Kosei's intense expression. Kosei painfully grabbed Maiku's shoulder, kneading them between clenched fingers, and stared into his eyes.

"Maiku-ie, what just happened here?"

Tubaki threw open the door to the student council room without knocking. She slammed the door and leaned against it. Her back moved up and down on the sliding door with each heaving breath she took. She slouched down into a sitting position and rested her head on her knees. Ichigo was sitting in the president's chair reading the instruction manual to an eavesdropping device she bought from the Home Shopping Network. She could not help feeling surprised at Tubaki's actions.

"What… happened?" Ichigo said, hesitantly. She was not usually one to do anything hesitantly. Tubaki's shoulders shook. She had not realized that anyone else was in the room.

"Ms. President," Tubaki said, looking up. She gave Ichigo a needy look and stood up. She carefully walked to the president's seat, as unsteadily as a blind person. Ichigo jumped up from her seat and rushed to Tubaki's side. She looked as though she might collapse at any second.

"You'll be fi…" Ichigo started, but before she could get out the last word Tubaki reached out and held on to her small form. Ichigo's nose and mouth seemed blocked by Tubaki's massive chest. Tubaki leaned all her weight into Ichigo and wept bitterly.

"That's what happened. It was really sudden and I have no idea what's going on." Maiku was standing in the hall looking off where Tubaki had run. He had just quickly explained everything that happened to Kosei who then softened his grip on Maiku's shoulder.

"Wow. So that's what happened." Maiku noticed the unusually deep expression on Kosei's face and thought that just maybe…

"Shimazaki, do you maybe have an idea why she did that?"

"Yeah," Kosei nodded solemnly with an expression so serious that it was hard to believe he was the same Kosei Maiku knew.

"Tubaki? Are you feeling any better?" Ichigo asked Tubaki, who was squeezed into the president's seat with her. Tubaki was sitting facing Ichigo and nodded shyly like a young child. She had wiped away her tears and the only sign that she had been crying was the bit of red still visible around her eyes. Tubaki sipped a bit of tea from the glass in her hands.

"Would you like to tell me what happened?" Ichigo inquired. After a bit of hesitation Tubaki told Ichigo the reason for her sudden tears.

"I used to have a little brother. Or I guess I should say I almost had a little brother."

It was six years ago, when Tubaki was eleven years old that her mother was pregnant. As an only child who had always wanted a little brother or sister, it was all she had ever dreamed of. Her father was exceedingly happy to find out they were going to have a baby boy. Before her mother even started to look pregnant, the members of the Oribe home were getting ready to welcome their first boy. They bought all blue baby clothes and lots of toys for the soon-to-be newest member of their family. Tubaki, who did everything she could to help, was excitedly awaiting the birth of her new baby brother. As her mother's stomach got bigger and bigger Tubaki became more and more excited, telling her mother "I'm going to do this with my brother." "I'm going to be a big sister, so I'll have to look after him." "I'll share my snacks with him." "I'll make sure no one tries to bully him." Her mind was full of ideas of what to do when her brother was born.

However, the door to being a four member family was heartlessly shut off to them mere seconds after it was opened. The unborn child that was to be Tubaki's little brother had a congenital heart defect and died just 47 seconds after his birth. All of the doctors' efforts had no effect and the child passed away without even crying. The parents, who were so looking forward to holding their new child, only got to hold a new unvarnished box that held the child's remains in an urn so small it brought tears to their eyes.

Fortunately, the mother made a full recovery. She had her health, but Tubaki's mother's loss was great and she suffered because of it. The Oribe home was veiled in sadness and for a long time no one laughed at all. It seemed as if they would never get over their grief, but, as they say, time heals all wounds. They gradually suppressed all of the painful memories and eventually were able to act as if they had forgotten it all.

Tubaki met Kosei when she was in 8th grade, three years after her brother's death. Kosei was a new student at the time, and joined the literature club, of which Tubaki was a member. At first their relationship was no more than that of two members of the same club, but after a year they became intimate friends. Kosei thought of himself and Tubaki as boyfriend and girlfriend. She thought the same, at least until that happened.

One day Tubaki, Kosei and several other club members were staying after school to edit their club publication. As it got closer to go home, one student left, then two others, and before they realized it Tubaki and Kosei were alone in the room lit by the late afternoon sun. Kosei was first to notice they were alone. Tubaki was sitting across the table from Kosei busily checking over the publication draft. Tubaki's hair was much shorter then and the side that was facing the window was beautifully lit in a clear orange color from the sun.

Kosei stopped working and, because it seemed natural, leaned in close to kiss her. They had never kissed before. Unlike many other middle school students these days, it was not until after one year of dating that they had finally held hands. Tubaki looked up as she noticed him approaching and was surprised at how close his face was. She pulled back the slightest bit.

"Kosei."

"You don't want to?" That was all Kosei had to say. Tubaki knew what he wanted to do.

"Well, we're only in middle school."

"Don't you mean we're already in middle school?" Kosei was annoyed at the hesitation of his older girlfriend. He was more than ready for his first kiss.

"Don't you like me, Tubaki?" He only called her by her first name when they were alone. Tubaki finally realized that they were now alone in the classroom.

"Of course I like you, it's just…"

"Then why not?" Kosei put his hands on her shoulders.

What should I do? What should I do? What should I do?

Tubaki was going back and forth between her options. But as she was debating with herself over what to do, Kosei's lips were getting closer.

Yeah. We've been going out for a while, it's OK to just kiss him…

She prepared herself for the kiss and closed her eyes, but when their lips were mere millimeters from touching she was suddenly over-whelmed by a strange feeling. If she had to put it into words, it was that this was "wrong." She could not put her finger on exactly why, but the feeling moved her to turn her face from Kosei's, pushing him away. The question, "Why?" was written all over Kosei's face, and even Tubaki did not know the answer.

"I'm sorry, I just… can't…"

"Why not?" Kosei asked, the awkwardness and confusion of the situation made his voice sound angry. Tubaki started to cry. As the tears poured down her face she slowly began to understand why it was "wrong."

She had, until just seconds ago, thought of Kosei as her lover. Maybe that was too strong of a word for someone she had not even kissed. She could probably have called him her boyfriend. It was fun being with Kosei. She felt relaxed around him. She could talk about any-thing with him and wanted him to talk about everything with her. If he felt angry or sad, she would feel the same way. She did not want to see him cry, so she would try to do something to make him feel happy. She felt all of these things for her lover who was a year younger than her. She believed that and never once doubted it. But that was just an illusion.

The feelings that Tubaki had for Kosei was a type of love. But not the love you feel for your boyfriend, it was the love you felt for your family, like the feelings one had toward a brother. Basically, Kosei was just a substitute for the brother that Tubaki never had. She thought that time had healed those wounds, and even she was unaware that the pain was still very real inside her heart. Perhaps it was because her mother had grieved the loss of her only son so deeply that Tubaki felt she must put on a happy face and hide her own grief. She buried the feelings deep within her heart and the wounds had not been allowed to heal, so instead they kept bleeding, fostering the desire to seek a substitute for that life that had expired after only 47 seconds.

When they first met, Tubaki had wondered why she was so drawn to Kosei. Kosei had just started middle school, and tried very hard to hide his childishness, but that made it even more obvious. He spoke politely, but every once in a while he showed a bit of his irreverent side and would seem very uneasy. He was not the type who made people act protective of him, but when one noticed the fragility beneath his adult-like surface, it was impossible to take one's eyes off him. He was a perfect example of boys at that transitional age.

If my brother had lived he might have been just like this...

If Tubaki's brother had lived he would have only been three years old at this time so it was impossible to imagine that he would be just like Kosei. But because she had never even touched her real brother, she felt free to imagine and soon had an image of how her brother would have turned out. For Tubaki, going out with Kosei was like spending time with the brother she never had. But even Tubaki herself was unaware of this fact, and Kosei was just a member of the opposite sex who was developing feelings for her. It was only natural that Kosei would want to kiss her if he had the chance. But when Kosei crossed the line by attempting something taboo between brother and sister, the happiness they once shared crumbled to pieces because they were each coming into the situation with different intentions.

When Tubaki realized the real reason behind the feelings that she had mistaken for love, she explained to Kosei, through her tears, why she refused to kiss him. It was very sudden, unexpected, and hard for Kosei to accept. He sat, bathed in the sunlight, in front of the sobbing Tubaki and, not knowing what else to do, lapsed into silence, balling up his hands.

The next day Kosei dropped out of literature club and he and Tubaki never saw each other thereafter. Tubaki's graduation and change of schools made her start to think of the time she spent with Kosei as just another memory of younger days and she pushed them aside to the back of her mind.

"That really happened?" Ichigo said, taking a sip of her now cold tea. "So you must have been really surprised when Shimazaki came to this school."

"Not really, I was sort of expecting him to."

It was not unexpected that Kosei, given that he did not choose a private school, would come to this school because it was in the same district as his public middle school. Plus, regardless of the truth of the situation, Tubaki thought she had dealt with her feelings about Kosei. When she started her second year of high school, rather than worry about her past with him, she was more interested in other things. Like the new student in Kosei's class, Maiku Kamishiro.

She had joined the student council and through her activities with Ichigo she had gained access to machines that contained data about every student. One that had particularly interested her was Maiku's. An orphan raised in an institution, who now did free-lance computer programming to earn his living. Her curiosity was aroused by his strange situation.

She met Maiku many times when she accompanied Ichigo on her trips to try to convince him to join the student council. As she saw him more often, this unsociable, blunt freshman began to occupy a big space in her mind. Tubaki, realizing this, thought with confidence that she had found a new love.

"But I was wrong. It's just the same as before…" Tubaki whispered, dejectedly. She looked down at her now empty tea cup.

It had been wrong again. What she thought was love had only been an illusion. She was just imagining Maiku as the brother she never had.

He is just like a brother…

Strangely, the same thought that had popped into her head when she was in a similar situation with Kosei (the situation that had lead to their breakup), made her realize that she was making the same mistake with Maiku. The feelings she had for Maiku were not love. She could tease young naïve guys by showing off her well-developed body, but she could not kiss them to show love, much less consider doing anything more. Even plainly showing off her sex appeal to Maiku at the beach was something maybe she was only able to do because somewhere inside she was thinking of him as a brother. It seemed strange to consider, but maybe she was not bothered by Miina and Karen because she considered them her rivals in love, but because she thought of them as pests who were tempting her dear brother.

"I thought that maybe… maybe things would work out with Kamishiro," Tubaki said, sniffing, "He's a student, but he works and supports himself. He seems so much more mature than the other kids…"

"So you thought you would never think of him as a little brother," Ichigo offered as Tubaki trailed off.

"This is obvious, but he is a freshman so he's still younger than me."

There are many couples in which the woman is older than the man, and only one year is not a whole lot of difference. But Tubaki was surprised to find that the guy she fell for after Kosei would also be younger.

"It's as if time stopped that day my brother died. Six years have passed and I still haven't recovered from it…"

"Like time has stopped…" Tubaki could not see, but under the table Ichigo was making fists so tight that her nails were digging into the palms of her hands.

"Ms. President, what should I do?

"I'm sorry, but this problem is within you and there is nothing I can do to help." Ichigo looked into Tubaki's desperate eyes with a cold stare. "And there's only one thing I can tell you." Tubaki stared intently at Ichigo's mouth waiting to see what she would say. "Move on," Ichigo said, curtly, but resolutely. "No matter how hard things get you can't just let things stop. You have to move on. you know that, right? Just keep moving on."

"But…" Tubaki tried to find the words, but Ichigo interrupted.

"I don't know where or how you should move on. It's difficult to choose the right path. You will probably get lost along the way. But even though finding the path is difficult, moving on is easy. You just have to be brave and just take a step forward."

"I just have to take a step forward?"

"Yeah, so please don't stop, just move on." There was a surprising amount of feeling in Ichigo's usually monotonous voice. Quite a surprise, actually. Tubaki gave a little nod, her eyes still full of tears.

Kosei and Maiku headed back to the conference room and Kosei told Maiku all about his past with Tubaki. Maiku was so surprised he did not know what to say at first. He thought he should say something, but had no idea what.

"I think Tubaki must have realized," Kosei continued, trying to relieve some of the awkwardness they felt, "that her feelings for you were not love."

"You think so?" The story he had just heard was so unbelievable he was having difficulty accepting it. He could not even believe that Tubaki and Kosei had been going out in middle school in the first place. He probably would have thought it was some bad joke, if it were not for the serious expression on Kosei's face.

Wait a second, if they were going out that means...

"Kosei, so you actually..." Kosei figured out what Maiku was trying to say without hearing it all.

"Yeah. I actually like girls."

"Then why...?"

"I guess I wouldn't go as far to call it an aftereffect, but after what happened with Tubaki I've been kinda afraid to go out with girls."

"Afraid?"

"Like, no matter how much I like a girl, and even if I think she likes me, it might just be my imagination. I feel like it must be an illusion that we share the same feelings and that at the last minute she'll betray me."

94

"Shimazaki…" Maiku made a pained expression when he thought of how badly the situation with Tubaki had hurt Kosei.

"But, I'm popular without even trying because I'm good looking," Kosei added to lighten the situation.

"Uh..."

An incredibly vague expression appeared on Maiku's face.

"So in middle school a lot of girls in my class and even underclassmen asked me out, but I really didn't want to go out with anyone. It was so annoying to keep saying no, so when I got to high school I just started acting like I wasn't interested in girls. That way no girls would think of me as someone they'd like to go out with."

Kosei ignored Maiku who looked like he wanted to say something. "I chose you as my target because for one, you had the seat next to mine, and because you seemed like the kind of guy who would make a good target. It seemed totally likely that we could be a couple."

Maiku did not know what to say to that.

"Maiku-ie, I really feel bad about this. I know it must be annoying what with all the rumors about us…"

"Shimazaki? Are those really the only reasons you chose me for a target?"

"Huh?" Kosei looked confused, but soon his mouth twisted. "If you're saying you think I stayed close to you to make sure nothing happened between you and Tubaki, you're wrong. That was just a coincidence. But it's ironic, isn't it? That Tubaki and I both chose you as the pseudo object of our affections."

"Are you telling the truth?" Maiku asked, looking Kosei straight in the eye.

"You just won't give it up! I keep telling you that wasn't the reason. It really wasn't, at first," Kosei let slip.

"So was it when you realized?" Maiku was quick to ask.

"Well…" Maiku turned his eyes from Maiku's face. Just as his expression had almost returned to its usual playfulness, it turned dark again. "Yeah, that probably influenced me, but I didn't even realize it myself. No, maybe I did. I think somewhere inside I was jealous. I hoped it wouldn't work out."

"Shimazaki, do you still like her?"

"It's pathetic, I know. Clinging to a love that ended a long time ago. And to Tubaki it wasn't even love," Kosei smiled at his own foolishness.

"Are you really OK leaving things like this, Kosei?" Maiku questioned him.

"Of course not!" Kosei's tone was surprisingly strong.

"Then why?"

"Because it's over. Everything between us is over!" Kosei spit out.

"So why don't you try it again!" Maiku said loudly, not giving up.

"Try again?"

"Yeah. Who says you only get one chance and then it's 'game over'? There's no rule like that in love.

"But… but Tubaki only thinks of me as a little brother…"

"So what? Even if she treats you that way, it's not like you're related. You can get past it!"

"Maiku-ie…" Kosei whispered and suddenly leaned forward

and hugged Maiku who was sitting across from him.

"Whoa!"

"Thank you, Maiku-ie!" Kosei tightened his grip around Maiku's body. "I think I really am going to fall for you!"

"Please try to control yourself…"

Kosei released Maiku from his grip and stood up, full of energy.

"I'm gonna go find Tubaki."

"She might have already gone home."

"Then I'll go look at her house," Kosei said as he left the conference room. In his mind Maiku gave him a cheer as he watched him leave.

That's right, Shimazaki. Tubaki isn't related to you so your love might blossom.

"Not actually related…" Maiku whispered to himself as he sat alone in the classroom, bathed in the late afternoon sun.

"What? A girl when running out of the room crying?" Karen blanched as she watched Marie's gesture report from the usual place in the sitting room after work. "Then she was hugging a guy…"

"What happened?" Miina asked as she watched the two communicate through strange gestures. Karen looked very serious.

"It seems that something nasty… I mean ghastly has happened."

"Something ghastly?"

"Well, the particulars are a bit complicated so I'm not exactly sure what…" It seemed that some things are not possible to convey through gestures.

"Then I guess we'll have to ask him, won't we."

"Yes. I want to know exactly what happened."

They decided to bring it up at dinner.

"Maiku, did something happen today after school?"

"Please be honest." Maiku who was sipping tea in the sitting room between Miina and Karen looked at them with a puzzled expression.

"What do you mean 'something'?"

"That's what we're asking!" Miina said with such intensity she almost banged her fist on the low table. "We know something happened. There's no use hiding it."

"Yeah. We heard from our secret spy report so we know something happened," added Karen trying her hardest to look stern.

"Secret spy? What are you talking about?" Maiku furrowed his brow at this strange word.

"Don't change the subject!" Miina said leaning in toward Maiku.

"Tell us the truth. Did something happen today or not?"

"Now that you mention it, I guess something did..." Maiku said, carelessly as Miina and Karen surrounded him with intense expressions on their faces. The two girls started making a huge fuss, like two drugged up gamecocks.

"I knew it! You did something nasty with that hoochie girl with glasses!"

"That's disgusting, Maiku! You're not over 18! That's for adults!"

"You idiots, I just said something happened today, I didn't mean anything like that!" Maiku set down his teacup and stood up with an expression that seemed to say, 'I don't know how I put up with you two.'

Miina and Karen yelled after him as he walked out of the sitting room.

"Trying to run away, huh?"

"Maiku, please explain what happened!" Karen implored.

"You can't say it, can you?! It's something you can't explain, isn't it!"

"Oh no! You don't think he did unspeakable things, do you?!"

Maiku headed up to his room, ignoring Miina and Karen and letting them think whatever deluded thoughts they wanted to think. He went inside and leaned against the sliding door without even turning on the lights. He sat there thinking about all the things he had been through that day, and whispered to himself.

It was nothing like that. Not at all.

Chapter 9: Mic Performance

"Oh, it's Ms. Mizuho!" It was Saturday after school and Miina and Karen had been on cleaning duty. They had just finished their work and were heading home when they saw Mizuho Kazami at the school entrance.

"Are you going home now, Ms. Mizuho?" Karen asked.

"Yes, I am," Mizuho answered, nodding.

They all lived in the same direction so the three of them walked together for a while, making small talk. Just as they had passed through one neighborhood, too small to even be called a residential area, they heard lively music and saw a festival float coming around the corner. On the float that was carried by men wearing happi, there were children dressed in traditional clothes and awkwardly playing flutes and drums.

"A float? There must be a festival today," Mizuho whispered as she saw the float going by them on the street. Then she said to Miina and Karen, "By float, I don't mean that drink with soda and ice cream."

"I don't think there is anyone who would think you did, considering the circumstances," Miina said calmly in response to Mizuho's comment that really could not even be considered a joke.

"Yeah, I guess you're right. Who would make a stupid mistake like that?" Mizuho said, hurriedly. Then she pointed at the children on the float that was slowly moving out of sight. "Would some people maybe worry that those children would be sacrificed during the festival?"

"No."

"Definitely not." Miina and Karen assured her with their quick responses.

"Oh, I see."

She is really beautiful and very kind, but there's something weird about her.

That same thought was running through both Miina and Karen's minds. She was like someone from a far off country, often not knowing things that any Japanese person would, or making really strange mistakes.

Mizuho, noticing the strange looks on their faces, walked ahead to the intersection and pointed to the right.

"I live over there. I'll see you later."

Miina and Karen quickly said goodbye to the teacher as she hurriedly turned the corner. They watched her leave with looks of confusion on their faces.

"A festival?" Maiku asked, holding his chopsticks over his bowl. He stared at Miina, who was sitting on his right.

"Yeah. It looks like a nearby shrine is having a summer festival. Why don't we go after dinner?"

"I'm not a kid. I don't really want to go." Maiku made a half-hearted expression and Karen, who was on his left, leaned forward.

"You don't like festivals, Maiku?"

"It's not that I don't like them…"

"Then let's go!" Miina said, as if she was ready to jump up that very second.

"If you want to go so much, why don't just the two of you go?"

"Jeez! Why are you always so unsocial like that? That's why you don't have many friends!"

"Leave me alone," Maiku gave them an annoyed look and irritably bit into the fried shrimp in his chopsticks.

"Come on Maiku, don't be like that! Let's gooo!" Karen said, pestering Maiku.

"We haven't spent much time together recently since you've been so busy with the concert planning. The three of us should go out!" Miina said, eagerly.

"We just went to the beach, didn't we?"

"That was forever ago!"

"It was just recently," Maiku said curtly. Miina turned on the tatami, still holding her chopsticks, and started kicking her feet like a spoiled child.

"I wanna go! I wanna go! I wanna go to the festival!!"

The dishes were shaking on the table and miso soup was about to spill from some of the bowls.

"Hey! Cut it out!" Even when Maiku tried to sound empathetic, Miina ignored him and kept on with her temper tantrum. Then Karen put her hands together and gave Maiku a pleading look.

"Please, Maiku! This summer's festival will only happen this summer!"

"Well, yeah…" Maiku realized he was not going to stop them unless he went. He sighed and said, "Fine, fine. I'll take you."

Miina and Karen immediately sat up straight and put their arms in the air saying, "Yay!"

Maiku, thinking 'jeez,' looked at them sternly and said, "But you only get 1000 yen ($10) each."

"Wow, there are so many people!" Karen said, expressing her

reaction to the number of people walking along the path to the shrine just past the torii (gateway).

"Yeah, it's even livelier than I was expecting!" Miina agreed, nodding.

Contrary to the rural, small festival the girls and even Maiku were expecting, the stone-paved path was lined with street stalls on both sides. It was more packed than the city on a weekend. As they went through the torii and walked onto the path, the festival music and voices they had heard before became even louder. The uncovered light bulbs that were strung on a cord from the poles of the stalls seemed to sweep away the darkness. There was the smell of rich yakisoba sauce, soy sauce baste cooking on fried corn on the cob, the sweet scent of mini sponge cakes, and so many other wonderful smells mixed together and flooded their senses from both sides of the path.

Miina, who was wearing a bright yellow dress, kept looking back and forth.

"Oh! Takoyaki (octopus balls)… another over here there are candy apples! Mmm cold pineapple sounds good,too!"

"Miina, you just ate!" Karen chided. She was wearing a white short-sleeved blouse with a light blue jumper over it.

"But they say you have a separate stomach for food you buy at a festival."

"No one says that!" pointed out Maiku, who was wearing a white open-necked shirt and linen pants. His ensemble was quite similar to his school uniform.

"Let's just walk around first. We'll get something to eat after that," Karen said, being unexpectedly reasonable.

"What? Come on! Don't be such a goody-two shoes!" Miina said, pouting.

"No," Karen replied curtly. "Don't say I didn't warn you if you feel sick after eating too much."

Maiku walked along with the flow of the crowd thinking, "Even after walking around, if you ate as much as Miina does I bet you would feel sick." When they got to the shrine pavilion at the end of the path, there was already another couple standing there, but they soon left and Maiku and the two girls took their places in front of the wooden box for money offerings. Maiku threw in a five yen coin and wished for luck and Miina rang the bell vigorously. If there were any gods resting, that definitely roused them.

Maiku put his hands together and said a prayer. When he opened his eyes he saw that Miina and Karen, standing on either side of him, still had their eyes closed and looked very serious. The two opened their eyes at almost the same time, and after having made Maiku wait for so long he was starting to feel uncomfortable. When they left, a family took their place.

"What did you wish for?" Miina asked, walking up close to Karen.

"It... it's a secret."

"That's awful suspicious." Miina thought it was very strange that Karen had startled and stiffened when she asked. "It wasn't anything that would go against the codes of our love alliance, was it?" Miina asked looking at Karen's face from the side.

"No! Definitely not!"

"You seem a little too defensive about that..." Miina said, and

Karen's cheeks flushed.

"What about you, Miina? Did you wish for something against the code, maybe?"

"Wha?" Miina was momentarily caught of guard by Karen's counterattack. "N-no! Of course not!"

"Then tell me what you wished for."

"I, uh…I wished for world peace," Miina answered, turning away.

"Really?" Karen looked at Miina's face from the side.

"What are you guys doing?" Maiku turned around to ask. They ran to his side like two dogs that had been called by their master's whistle.

"Hey Maiku, what did you wish for?" Miina asked. Maiku dodged the question by pretending he didn't hear her and weaved through the crowd back toward where they had come in. He turned to the girls who were sticking close to his side.

"If we get separated we'll meet by the torii at the entrance, got it?"

"OK!" Miina answered casually. Maiku nodded and turned to Karen on his other side.

"You be especially careful if you get separated."

"I… I'm not a little child! I won't get lost... Oh! Little chicks!"

Karen ran over to the chick-catching stand she noticed and immediately forgot what they had been talking about. She crouched down near the stand and looked down at all the little chicks that were crowded in the corners of a case that was about five square feet. There was one chick that was not with the group, as if it had something else to do, and it started hopping over to Karen.

"Ooo, it's a little chick! It's so tiny, and soft, and it's chirping!" she said in an animated voice. Karen thought it was strange that no one was responding to the obvious statements she had just rattled off, and she turned her head to look. But Maiku and Miina, who she had expected would be right behind her, were no where to be seen. She stood up and looked around.

"Where are they?" she said, tilting her head in confusion.

"Hey, Maiku." Miina called. Maiku was engrossed by a balloon stand where a man was sculpting long thin balloons into poodles in mere seconds with the utmost facility.

"What?" he said, turning to Miina.

"Karen's gone."

"What?!" Maiku looked around, expecting Karen to be following behind, but she was no where in sight. "Jesus, right after I told her to be careful," Maiku said hanging his head down and resting his right cheek on his hand.

"What should we do?" Miina asked.

"I dunno…" It would be impossible to find Karen in this crowd. Their best bet was to follow their plan and go wait for her by the torii.

"I guess we should just go back to the torii for now."

"I guess that's all we can do," Miina said, and walked next to Maiku with a frown on her face. She wanted to try to find Karen quickly, but in this crowd all they could do was walk at a speed somewhere between a shuffle and a slow crawl. But, even though she was spacey, Karen was a high school student, after all. She was too old to be lost and crying somewhere, so they were not too worried. Plus, as long as they waited by the torii they believed she would eventually come. In fact, Miina was so calm that she was even feeling lucky about her chance to be alone with Maiku.

It's like we're on a date...

She knew perfectly well that Maiku was not of the same mind, but the two of them walking through the festival crowd on this summer night... to an outsider it would surely look like a date. Miina pushed aside an image of Karen looking around worriedly for them. She was secretly thankful for Karen's absent-mindedness.

"Hey, Miina?"

Maiku's suddenly saying her name gave Miina a start because she had been day dreaming about things that were clearly in violation of the love alliance codes.

"Wh... what?"

"Are you thirsty?"

"I... uh, not really." Miina's guilty conscience had made her panic for no reason.

"Oh, then wait a minute," Maiku said, and walked over to the side of the path where a beach umbrella was set up. Maiku bought a drink that had been cooling in a bucket of ice from the man under the umbrella and came back.

"Hey."

"Huh? Oh, hi," Miina said, turning. She had been looking in the opposite direction of where Maiku had gone and looked a bit out of it. She seemed distracted by something and even when Maiku tried to start walking she made no effort to follow.

"What's wrong?" Maiku asked.

"Maiku, can we try it?" Miina asked, pointing at a ring toss stand.

"What? We should find Karen first.

"Yeah, but…"

"Come on, let's go."

"Please! Just once!" She put her hands together and looked at Maiku pleadingly.

"Miina…"

"Come on, you went and got a drink. I just want to do this once!"

"Fine, but just once," Maiku said, giving into her half-logical plea.

"Now you're talking!" Miina happily ran off toward the ring toss stand and impatiently pulled her wallet out of her dress pocket.

"I'd like to play!"

Maiku walked after her drinking his drink.

I guess it's ok…

There was no way Karen could get to the torii before them. It did not really matter if they passed the time here for a little while.

Miina paid the man running the stand and he handed her three rings made of bamboo covered in vinyl tape. There were cheap prizes laid out on a vinyl sheet on the ground in front of her. Miina aimed for a white cat stuffed animal with black spots that was sitting between a plastic model of Himeji Castle and a cheap-looking trophy. The first time, she threw it too hard, and it went past the cat's head. She aimed for the same prize with her next two rings, but she could not hit it and did not win a prize.

"You were real close," said Maiku, who was watching from behind her. Miina nodded feebly with her shoulders slouching in disappointment. "Did you want that stuffed toy that badly?" To Maiku it just looked like a cheap toy that one might find in a UFO catcher game and he did not understand why she would want it.

"I used to have a pet cat," Miina said quietly to no one in particular after they had been walking for a while. "That stuffed toy really looked like my cat."

"So that's why you wanted it."

"We only had it for about two or three days, actually," Miina said, with a depressed look, a complete change from her usual perky disposition.

"Did it run away?"

"No, she was abandoned," Miina said, grimacing as if remembering something unpleasant. "I had found her. It was a rainy day and she was in a cardboard box by the garbage cans. She was so tiny she could fit in the palm of my hand and she looked up at me and meowed. When I pet her head she rubbed up against me. I knew I'd get in trouble if I brought her home, since I was in foster care, but I just couldn't leave her there."

Perhaps Miina, who had been abandoned by her parents when she was too young to understand, somehow saw a bit of herself in the cat. She could not leave a young abandoned creature that was so similar to her.

"I tried to keep her hidden from them... the people who took me in. But in the end, they found out about her."

"Then what happened?"

"They told me to get rid of her. It was almost like they were saying, 'how can one abandoned creature care for another?'"

Maiku did not know how to respond to the painful story Miina was relaying to him. It was like seeing the deep scars in her heart.

"So I took the cat back to where I found it. I put a newspaper in the box so she wouldn't be cold and I tried to put the box where it wouldn't get drenched in the rain. But when I said goodbye and started to walk away, the kitten followed me. I kept saying, 'sorry, but I can't keep you at my house,' and put her back in the box. But she kept following me…" Miina felt a lump in her throat and could not finish. She kept her head down.

Maiku did not know what to say to her and a silence fell over the two of them as they walked through the lively crowd. Finally they reached the torii and Maiku looked around so pointedly that it seemed unnatural.

"Karen doesn't seem to be here yet, huh?"

"Yeah," Miina said in a slightly nasal voice. She put her hands on her hips and said, as if trying hard to sound upset, "Jeez, that girl sure is taking her sweet time!"

Maiku leaned against the torii and watched the people going by, searching for Karen among them. Then, as if he suddenly remembered something said, "Miina, wait here for a minute. I just remembered something I have to do."

"What?"

"It doesn't matter, just wait right here. I'll be right back."

Maiku strode off into the crowd so quickly that Miina did not even have a chance to try to stop him. Maiku wove through the crowds and soon arrived at the ring toss stand. Fortunately, the cat stuffed animal that Miina wanted was still there.

Thank God! No one got it.

Maiku paid the man and immediately set his eye on the cat toy sitting on top of the sheet. He threw the ring. It had not looked difficult, but it was actually quite hard and he completely missed his target. Maiku soon had thrown all of his rings so he took out his wallet. He soon ran out of rings again. It seemed like his eagerness to win the toy for Miina was not enough. He tried a third time, but he was unable to win the prize.

Maybe he just was not any good at the ring toss. He thought if he kept trying he would just waste his money. But he really wanted to win the toy for Miina. While Maiku was contemplating whether or not to try again, a ring thrown from beside him landed right on the cat stuffed animal. It was as if he was being mocked for his hesitation.

"Here you go. Nice job," the stand owner said apathetically, handing the stuffed toy to a woman in a yukata. The woman looked like she was in her mid-thirties and had long shiny hair that fell to her waist. She had full breasts that filled the front of her yukata and made deep cleavage peaking out from the V of the neckline. She gave off the intense sexiness of an adult woman.

"It's so cute!" she said looking at the stuffed cat the stand owner had handed her.

Maiku looked dejected, having had his prize taken right from under his nose. He gaped at the woman as she walked away holding the toy in one hand.

"Excuse me!" Maiku called after her, without even thinking.

"Yes?" she said, turning toward him. Maiku's heart started racing, as he realized that he had actually called out to her.

"I... this, uh may seem sudden, but I was um… wondering if you would let me have that stuffed animal you just won…"

At first the woman looked confused at the request from this unfamiliar boy, but then she lightly waved the toy in her hand and said, "This?"

"Ye-Yes. I would be willing to pay you for it."

"It seems that you really want it."

"Well… yes."

The woman looked at Maiku as if she was trying to size him up. "I'll give it to you, but on one condition."

"Condition?"

"I'm really bored all by myself here. If you'll stay with me for a while, I'll give it to you."

"Wha…?" Maiku was speechless for a second at the woman's request that had been even stranger than his own.

"So? I think it's a pretty good deal."

"But, what do you mean by stay with you?"

"I'm not asking you to sleep with me or anything. Just walk around the festival with me for a while."

It may have been unexpected, but it was not a bad deal. He probably would have agreed to it right away if he had not been keeping Miina waiting at the torii.

"If you really don't want to, I won't make you," the woman said, looking as if she was going to leave, when Maiku did not answer.

"OK. I'll do it," Maiku said hurriedly.

"Then it's a deal!" she said, coming up next to Maiku and putting her arm in his. Her warm chest was pushed up against his elbow.

"Um… I… uh..."

"What?" the woman asked innocently, even though she knew exactly what was making Maiku nervous. She smiled at him seductively and said, "You said you'd stay with me, right?"

After they had walked a few steps, arm in arm, she said, "You know, we haven't even introduced ourselves yet!"

"Oh, my name is Maiku Kamishiro."

"I'm Hatsuho. Hatsuho Kazami."

"Kazami?" Maiku thought of his homeroom teacher when he heard the familiar name.

Come to think of it, this woman even kind of looks like Ms. Mizuho...

"Ms. Hatsuho… are you by any chance related to Ms. Mizuho?"

"Oh! Are you one of Mizuho's students?" So she was related to Ms. Mizuho somehow.

"So are you Ms. Mizuho's older sister then?"

"You're such a nice kid," she said, smiling.

"What?" Maiku said, looking at her blankly.

She ignored his look and dragged him to a nearby takoyaki stand.

"I'll treat you to takoyaki."

"But…" Maiku was about to protest, but a high-spirited voice interrupted him from across the grill covered in iron cooking sheets with spherical indentations.

"What can I get you?" said the girl who looked like a middle school student, no doubt watching the stand for her parents. She quickly turned the takoyaki with an awl-like tool. She had her hair braid-

ed in two thick braids and was wearing glasses with round lenses. She had a few freckles across her nose. All in all she was a very agreeable-looking girl.

"One takoyaki, please," Hatsuho said, making her order.

"Sure thing," the girl responded cheerfully, "I'm cooking them up right now, so it'll just be a minute." She sized up Maiku and Hatsuho from behind the stand curtains as she expertly turned the takoyaki. "When I first saw you two I thought you looked a little too close in age to be mother and son, a little too far apart to be brother and sister... so tell me, are you guys actually... you know..." the girl said in a heavy Osaka accent, raising her eyebrows at Hatsuho.

"Oh! You figured us out!" Hatsuho said, putting her hands on her cheeks and squirming about nervously.

"So how is it having a young catch like that?" the girl asked, sounding much beyond her years.

"It's great! He had silky skin, and he's hard down there, if you know what I mean. He pleasures me every night with his never-ending supply of sperm."

"Wow, it sounds like you've found a great kid."

"But sometimes he has no restraint."

"For example?"

"He's always wants it! Like just a bit ago he suddenly said he wanted to 'do it,' so he took me behind the shrine yards. He did it hard from behind, standing up..."

"Whoa, aren't you two vivacious!"

"Wh... wait a minute! Stop making things up!" Maiku looked pale as he tried to cut into the conversation. He was interrupted by the package of takoyaki that the girl was pushing toward his face.

"Here ya go." She had been cooking while talking to Hatsuho. Hatsuho took the package with one hand and grabbed Maiku's arm with the other.

"Let's go." They walked away from the stand, making room for the next customers in line.

"What were you thinking?!" Maiku snapped at her.

"It was just a harmless joke," said Hatsuho, keeping her cool.

"A joke?"

While Maiku was staring at her dumbfounded, Hatsuho used a toothpick to pop a takoyaki into her mouth.

"Ish weally good." She blew on the piping hot takoyaki then poked another one with a toothpick and held it out toward Maiku's mouth. "Here you have some, they're really good!" Hatsuho kept pestering him, and Maiku took the takoyaki.

They are really good.

The takoyaki that girl with the Osaka accent had made were really quite delicious. The outside was crisp, but the center was soft and the rich sauce complimented it beautifully. This must be how authentic takoyaki taste. The octopus pieces were tough, but not too big and they accented the breading perfectly.

"Open up and say 'Ahhh'" Hatsuho said, bringing another takoyaki to Maiku's mouth. Maiku opened his mouth, feeling embarrassed doing something like this in public. Maiku had no idea that across the crowd there were two eyes open wide in shock at seeing him.

What should I do? I got separated from Maiku and Miina...

While Maiku and Miina were standing at the ring toss, Karen was wandering through the crowd of people alone. As soon as she realized she was alone she should have gone straight to the torii, but she was so upset she could not think straight. As she walked haphazardly through the crowd looking for Maiku and Miina, the shadow of worry in her mind grew larger and larger.

Where could they have gone? Why can't I find them? Maybe it's because they went somewhere together and left me on purpose...

Even though she knew that was not the case, the stone of doubt had been cast into the lake of her mind and distorted ripples were spreading from where it had hit the surface.

Maiku: It looks like we did it.

Miina: It's just the two of us now.

Maiku: I wonder if Karen will be OK alone...

Miina: Don't worry about her. She'll come home if she gets hungry.

Maiku: I guess you're right.

Miina: Since it's just the two of us, why don't we do something fun.

Without thinking, Karen yelled out loud at the image of Miina and Maiku "doing something fun" that vividly came into her mind.

"N-no! Miina! You're violating our love alliance codes!"

Oops...

Karen came to her senses at the sound of her voice and noticed the people who had stopped to see what was going on and were now staring at her. Her ears turned bright red in embarrassment. She tried to run away quickly, but in her hurriedness she bumped into a customer standing in front of the candy stand.

"Oh, excuse me…" she looked at the person's face and gulped in the middle of her apology. "Hoo…" She started to say 'hoochie girl with glasses' automatically when she saw Tubaki Oribe standing in front of her, but she quickly corrected herself and said, "Ms. Vice-President."

"You're that girl who lives with Kamishiro," Tubaki said and Kosei Shimazaki, who was standing next to her, looked over at Karen.

"Oh! Charlie, you're here, too?" Karen's eyes widened in surprise at seeing the two of them together.

"Why Charlie?" said Tubaki, looking over at Kosei.

"Because my first name is Kosei." Tubaki, who was used to Kosei's usual nonsense, ignored his incomprehensible logic.

"You're not with Kamishiro?" asked Tubaki, looking back at Karen.

"We came together, but I got separated from him and Miina."

"Oh, really?"

"I've been looking for them, but I can't find them anywhere."

"Did you have any meeting place planned in case you got separated?" Tubaki asked. With those words Karen finally remembered what Maiku had said.

"Yes, we did! He said to meet by the torii!"

"You should have thought of that in the first place," said Tubaki, looking surprised that Karen had not remembered something so simple.

"Well, I guess I should get going…" Karen wanted to go to the meeting place now that she finally remembered where it was.

"Yes. If you see Kamishiro…" Tubaki started to say, but Karen turned away and headed into the crowd before she got a chance to hear the rest. She left her worries behind and started walking quickly toward the torii. However, before she even got to the meeting place, she noticed Maiku standing across the crowd from her.

"Maiku…" Karen's face lit up as she started to call out to Maiku, but he started walking away toward the takoyaki stand. She noticed an unfamiliar older woman snuggling up next to Maiku in a very friendly manner.

Huh? Who could that be?

Considering how friendly they were with each other it could not be a stranger. Karen froze in place. She had assumed Maiku would be with Miina, so what could this possibly mean?

The mysterious woman was flirting with and clinging to Maiku, feeding him takoyaki as if she were trying to show off. To an outsider they seemed like a couple with an age gap, and their actions certainly suggested they were not your average pair. Karen, who was used to thinking of Tubaki, with her body that constantly reminded one of her appeal as a woman, as a rival, could not help but think there was something immoral about this unidentified woman who seemed to be oozing sex appeal from every pore of her body.

Could Maiku be doing unspeakable things with this woman? Like… I can't even think it!

An image that is unsuitable for good boys and girls under 18 was swirling around in Karen's mind. The thoughts were making her dizzy and her cheeks burned hot enough to melt butter. Karen, who did not have that much brain power to start with, felt like her mind was going to explode and she became dizzy. She began to stumble haphazardly and bumped into a woman who was walking behind her.

"Oh!" the woman said when Karen bumped into her. Then she looked at Karen and widened her eyes. "Onodera!"

Karen swung around in surprise and saw Maiku's homeroom teacher, Mizuho Kazami, standing behind her. Ms. Mizuho looked quite different from usual in a yukata with her hair done up and her glasses off.

Seeing someone she knew seemed to be the last straw for Karen's embarrassment threshold and everything around her started to go black.

"Wh…what's the matter?" Mizuho quickly caught Karen as her body crumpled toward her. She looked at Karen's closed eyes and said, "Oh my gosh, she's fainted again? Why? Why would seeing me make her faint?"

I have the feeling I've gotten myself caught up in something crazy here.

He was only supposed to stay with her for a little bit, but she kept dragging him from one stand to the next, and Maiku was getting pretty sick of it. It looked like the stuffed animal was going to cost him more than he had expected. Ignoring Maiku's desires to be released, Hatsuho noticed a large crowd of people in one corner of the shrine grounds.

"I wonder what's going on over there…" Hatsuho said, dragging Maiku in the direction of the throng of people. Just past the crowd there was a small stage set up and standing on it was a middle-aged man singing enka (classical Japanese) songs into a microphone. It looked like a karaoke contest.

The man finished his song and retreated to the edge of the stage to the sound of sparse applause. In his place appeared the MC who was wearing a sparkly tuxedo and a big bowtie. He came to the center of the stage carrying the microphone in one hand and looked over the audience.

"Alright! Now it's time for the customary volunteer singer from the audience! Is there someone out there who thinks they have the skills! Please raise your hand!"

Before he had even finished speaking Hatsuho's hand shot up in the air.

"Me!" The MC looked down at the white arm sticking out of a yukata sleeve.

"The beautiful woman in the yukata!"

"He called me beautiful," Hatsuho said trying to sound humble, but she was obviously pleased by the compliment. She happily started walking up to the stage.

"Uh…" Maiku started to say something, and she turned to him.

"Listen closely to what I sing, OK?"

"Uh… sure."

Hatsuho left Maiku standing there with the stuffed cat toy and climbed up the stairs to the shabby stage made with iron pipes. She smiled at the applauding audience, took the microphone from the MC and requested her song.

"I'll be singing 'Poppy Flower' by Agnes Chang."

She must like oldies because she certainly picked an old one. She swayed to the music as the introduction played. As soon as she had belted out the first words of the song into the microphone she was grasping in her hands, the audience shuddered. She was beyond tone-deaf; it was the most awful sound they had ever heard. It did not seem possible for any human to make that sort of sound. As if trying to stop her from continuing another second, the bell toned loud and clear.

Dooong!

The MC quickly ran onto the stage.

"Thank you very much! Now who wants to sing next?"

"What is the meaning of this? You have to let me sing the whole song!" Hatsuho insisted, but there would no doubt be casualties if they let her go on. Maiku watched Hatsuho screaming at the MC from the very back of the crowd. He did not think he wanted to spend any more time with her. He had done more than enough to pay her for the stuffed toy. So Maiku decided, and, feeling only a little guilty, he quietly snuck away.

What should I do now?

Mizuho sighed sitting in a rest area full of cushions under a tent on the corner where the path crossed. Mizuho was sitting on a cushion and next to her, leaning against one of the tent poles, was Karen who had passed out. Mizuho had somehow managed to carry Karen to the rest place after she had suddenly fainted. Karen did not open her eyes at all even when Mizuho called her name or lightly tapped her on the cheek. She was just running out of ideas when a cheerful voice called out to her.

"Hey, Ms. Mizuho!"

"Oh, it's you, Haruko."

She wore a mask askew on her face, was holding cotton candy in her right hand and a water balloon yo-yo in her left. It was fairly obvious that Haruko Shido was enjoying the festival to its fullest. She came up to Ms. Mizuho's side with her brother Matagu trailing behind her, like goldfish waste.

"Oh, Shido, you're here, too?"

"What's wrong with Karen?" Haruko asked, looking at her tired face.

"She suddenly fainted. I'm not really sure why."

"Not again!"

"I have to go find the friend I came with, but I really can't leave Karen like this."

"I'll stay and look after her!" said Haruko.

"You'd do that?"

"Sure! Matagu and I were just thinking of stopping to rest."

Mizuho looked and noticed that Matagu was holding a package of sunagimo kushiyaki from a yakitori stand and had a paper drink cup in each hand. It looked as if they were planning to eat in the rest area.

"Thanks, that would be great," Mizuho said standing up with a relieved look on her face, "I'll leave her in your care."

"Um, Ms. Mizuho?"

Mizuho, who had just left the tent, turned back to Matagu who had called after her.

"What is it, Shido?"

"You're not wearing your glasses today?"

"Uh, no. I didn't think they went well with a yukata," Mizuho answered, looking confused at his obvious question.

"What?! Glasses make any ensemble look more attractive! There are no clothes that don't look good with glasses! If it didn't look good for some reason you should change the clothes, not take off the glasses!" Matagu seemed crazy and spit flew as he gave his opinion that reeked of glasses-supremacism. Mizuho felt threatened and automatically stepped away from him. Haruko stepped forward from where she seemed to be hiding behind her pathetic brother and stood between them.

"Ms. Mizuho, just forget about this and get going. I'll give him a talking to."

"Oh… OK. Bye," Mizuho cut her pleasantries short and left, practically in a run.

Geez, he sure is taking his sweet time!

Miina was irritated standing alone by the torii, like she had been stood up for a date. Karen was off doing God knows what and had not shown up yet and Maiku still had not come back. Left alone, her thoughts began to wander. Soon horrible images were bubbling up in her mind.

I bet the two of them ran into each other somewhere and now…

Karen: Oh! Maiku!

Maiku: Karen! So here you are!

Karen: Ohhh, I was lonely all by myself!

Maiku: Hey now, don't hang all over me.

Karen: I'm sorry. I just am so happy to see you…

Maiku: Aww, alright.

Karen: Maiku, can we hold hands so I don't get lost again?

Maiku: That's a good idea. I wouldn't want you to get lost.

Karen: And it is just the two of us now… why don't we look around a bit more?

Miina became enraged by her own imagination and suddenly punched the torii with her fist.

"You better not!"

The people walking by turned to look at her. But Miina, moved by her own hallucinations, did not give them a second thought and ran into the crowd to look for Karen and Maiku.

"Unnn..." Karen groaned and slightly opened her eyes. She was leaning against a tent pole and Haruko and Matagu had just finished eating their chicken gizzard kebobs. Karen finally had come to. Matagu noticed and leaned over to her.

"Oh good, you're awake!"

"Ahhhhhhh!" Karen let out a piercing scream when she looked at Matagu's face right above her own.

Was that Karen?

Maiku was heading back to meet Miina at the torii with the stuffed toy in his hand when he heard Karen's scream. He immediately ran in the direction he heard it coming from. He pushed people out of his way as he ran toward the rest area and grabbed Matagu by the shirt. Matagu looked bewildered, having just been screamed at.

"What... what did you do to Karen?!"

"Wait a minute, Maiku."

"I'm fine, he didn't do anything yet," said Karen grabbing Maiku's arm, still not quite sure what had happened.

"Yet?" Matagu, still being held by the shirt, said, scrunching up his face in pain.

"I just was surprised when I opened my eyes and saw that creepy face looking at me," said Karen.

"That's right! It's just that Matagu is so gross and really tired looking. He wouldn't do anything worse than putting glasses on a sleeping girl," Haruko chimed in. Maiku finally seemed to calm down and took his hand from Matagu's shirt.

"Jeez, that was uncalled for," Matagu said looking at Maiku rue-fully and rubbing his neck a little too dramatically. Although his mistake was understandable considering the scream he heard, Maiku knew that he had jumped to conclusions.

"I'm sorry, Matagu," Maiku said bowing to Matagu.

"It's OK. As long as you know you were wrong."

Matagu may be a pervert, but he is good-natured at heart and was quick to forgive Maiku after his sincere apology. He was pleased to actually be respected as an upperclassman, since he so rarely got such treatment.

Haruko explained to Maiku that she and Matagu were looking after Karen for Ms. Mizuho, who had been with her when she fainted. Maiku thanked them both again and left with Karen. They headed to where Miina had been waiting. After they had been walking for a little while, Karen looked at Maiku with a serious expression on her face.

"Maiku, there's something I want to ask you."

"What?"

"Who was that woman you were with earlier?"

"Huh?" Maiku, caught off guard by the question, looked tense.

"I saw you. You were acting awful friendly with some woman."

"It… it must have been someone else."

"No. It was definitely you. I saw it clear as day." Maiku's uncomfortable appearance reassured her of any doubts she may have had.

"Karen, do you want to get something at a stand? You haven't gotten anything yet, have you?"

"Don't try to change the subject." Karen seemed even more sure of herself after Maiku's obvious attempt to dodge her question.

"Hmm, what should we get? How about cotton candy? You like sweet stuff, right?"

"Maiku!"

Maiku, pretending not to hear Karen, went to buy cotton candy from a nearby stand.

"Here, my treat."

"I won't be tricked like that!"

"You won't even have some after I went to the trouble of buying it?" Maiku said, popping some cotton candy into his mouth. He actually was not very fond of sweet things, but he tried to make a satisfied face. Karen started to look slightly interested.

Maiku put another piece in his mouth with a flourish and said, "You really don't want any? Then I'm gonna eat it all."

"No!" Maiku finally broke down Karen's defenses. "I want some too."

Maiku handed her the stick with the cotton candy on it and she quickly stuffed it in her mouth. She tore apart the sweet smelling fluff with her lips and her mouth was filled with the nostalgic sweet taste that was so different from that of chocolate or cake. A light expression spread across Karen's face. It was enough to even relax the expressions of those around her.

"It's so delicious!"

The cotton candy was enough to make her body and mind feel light and fluffy. Maiku was relieved by his apparent success at distracting her. Suddenly someone hugged him from behind, taking advantage of his letting his guard down.

"I found you!" Hatsuho said, poking her head around his shoulder and pressing her soft chest into his back.

"Ha-hatsuho!"

"You bad boy! Lighting a fire in my body and leaving me without saying a word!" Hatsuho whined in a nasal voice.

"What are you talking abo..." Maiku started to protest, but he felt someone burning through his head with her glare, and turned to the source with a grimace on his face. Karen had dropped her half-eaten cotton candy on the ground and was glaring at him.

"Maiku, who is this woman?"

"Uh, well... she's, uh... there's nothing between us. It's just... uh, well..."

"Nothing between us?! This from the boy who came three times!" Hatsuho said, continuing with her tiresome jokes. Karen, believed her, and a bright red blush spread all the way to her ears.

"You're dirty! You're a dirty pervert! You're breaking the Geneva Convention."

"No, you've got it wrong! Listen to me!" Maiku pleaded, the color draining from his face.

"You jerk!" Karen yelled and ran off. She seemed to have no interest in hearing him out.

"Hey!" Maiku tried to run after Karen, but Hatsuho had a tight grip on him. Maiku was trying to wriggle free from her hold when he heard a loud voice yell out from behind him.

"Ahh!"

Maiku and Hatsuho both turned to the source of the voice and saw Mizuho standing behind them.

"Oh, Mizuho…"

"Why are you with Kamishiro, mother?" Mizuho asked, sounding surprised.

"M- mother?!" This time it was Maiku's turn to be surprised. "I thought you were Ms. Mizuho's older sister!" he said staring at Hatsuho's face.

"I never said that."

She was right. When Maiku asked if she was Ms. Mizuho's sister she neither confirmed nor denied it. But there was no way Hatsuho could be over forty so it was only natural for Maiku to assume she was Mizuho's older sister.

"What were you thinking? Trying to mess around with one of my students, of all things!" Mizuho raised her eyebrows at her mother.

"I didn't do anything," said Hatsuho, smoothly moving away from Maiku.

"Are you OK, Kamishiro? Did she do anything horrible to you?"

"Come on, don't talk about me like I'm some sort of horny woman who's always in heat!"

"Oh, you're not?"

"I don't like your tone of voice! After I was nice enough to leave you alone with your husband. So this is what 'No child knows how dear she is to her parents' means."

"What? I was too busy worrying about you being somewhere up to no good that I couldn't even enjoy myself!"

"What a thing to say to your mother!"

It looked like the real fight was about to start so Maiku, not wanting to get caught in the middle, quietly slipped away. There was a part of him that wanted to tell Ms. Mizuho to keep her mother on a leash, but his first priority was finding Karen. He quickly headed off in the direction she ran. He had not taken ten steps when someone reached out from behind him and grabbed his shoulder firmly.

"Maiku!" Maiku turned to see Miina looking at him angrily. "Where were you?!"

"Miina? Why are you…"

"I'm the one who should be asking why you didn't come back! I gave up and came looking for you." Miina seemed pretty upset about being kept waiting for so long. She continued without giving Maiku a chance to speak. "What have you been doing all this time? I want an explanation…" she started to say when she noticed the cat stuffed animal from the ring toss in Maiku's hands. "You were getting that for me?"

"Yeah," Maiku nodded awkwardly and handed the toy to Miina.

"No way! Why…" Miina looked like she could not believe it as she reached out for the stuffed animal. She pulled it close to her chest.

Oh Maiku. I don't know if I'll be able to hold back my feelings after you've done this… after you've been so kind to me.

Miina was hugging the stuffed toy with her head hung down.

"Did you, uh… remember something unpleasant?"

"No, nothing like that! I'm just really touched that you did this for me."

"You're that touched?"

"No, really! I'm really happy!" Miina blushed when she realized how loudly she had proclaimed this.

"Oh… well, I'm glad then," Maiku said, turning away in embarrassment.

The mood was full of sweet embarrassment as they stood facing each other, seemingly unaware that they were still in the middle of a crowd.

"Maiku…" Miina started to say something to Maiku and an expression she had never shown spread across her face.

"Oh yeah!" Maiku suddenly yelled out.

"Wh- what?"

"I've gotta go after Karen!"

"What? You found her?"

"Yeah, but then she ran away."

"Huh? Why?"

"Well…"

He did not really have time to explain that Karen had misunderstood him when she saw his homeroom teacher's overly sexy mother hanging all over him. Plus, knowing Miina, his explanation might not be taken well.

"I'll explain later," Maiku said, heading in the direction Karen had gone. Miina followed him, holding the stuffed animal in one hand. She felt like she was walking on air.

Maiku got this for me. He did this for me!

Miina's mind was completely occupied with the stuffed animal from Maiku. She was supposed to be looking for Karen, but was not paying attention to anything around her. When she came to her senses for a second she realized that she had even lost sight of Maiku.

Uh-oh, I'm all alone again…

Karen trudged through the crowd alone with her head hanging.

Soon she was back in front of the chick-catching stand where she had first been separated from Maiku and Miina. The chicks, completely unaware of Karen's feelings, were chirping as they pushed and shoved in a large group. Karen was only half paying attention to them when her eyes fell on one chick that was waddling aimlessly away from the yellow group. She suddenly felt very sad when she realized the chick was a lot like her. She tried to hide the tingle in her nose by sniffing. The stand owner who was sitting behind the container where the chicks were playing looked up at her.

"What's wrong, miss?"

He looked like he was in his early forties. He had a square face and was wearing small sunglasses with round lenses and had a camel colored haramaki (stomach band) around his waist. He was dressed in a traditional manner that was rare even at festivals these days.

"You look down. Did you have a fight with your boyfriend?"

"N- no!" Karen quickly denied.

"Ha ha, it seems like I hit the nail on the head," laughed the man.

"No, really that's not it. It wasn't a fight or anything…"

"Miss," the man interrupted, seemingly uninterested in what she had to say.

"Did ya know that it's really hard to tell male and female chicks apart? Just sittin' here lookin' at 'em I haven't got a clue which is which. You've gotta look closely at the right parts to know for sure."

"Oh…" Karen, having no idea what the man was getting at, nodded half-heartedly.

"I think life is kinda like that. You don't know anything if you only look at it for a second. If ya actually take the time to listen to the other person and talk, ya find out, more often than not, you were mistaken about somethin'."

A mistake?

Karen thought about that for a minute. Earlier she ran off without listening to the explanation after she saw something shocking. Maybe, just maybe, there was some perfectly good, but complicated reason for it. Maiku had even said, 'Just let me explain.' Now that she thought about it, Maiku really would not do any of the horrible things she had thought of earlier. She had jumped to conclusions, but if she was able to just talk to him, maybe he could explain it. Yes, she was sure he could. Of course he could.

"That's right, people often do make mistakes," Karen whispered, reassuring herself. She turned to the stand owner with a cheery expression on her face, quite different from the one he had first seen.

"Thank you very much, Mr. Chick Stand Owner."

"I didn't do anything that deserves your thanks," he said, surprised by her straight thanks. He looked uncharacteristically shy, as if saying 'aw shucks.'

"Bye!" Karen said bowing slightly. She turned from the chick-catching stand and walked off with a bounce in her step.

I've got to find Maiku and talk to him. I'll have him explain what I saw earlier.

Karen was surprised by how light her step had become after deciding to go talk to Maiku. Karen walked aimlessly through the crowd for a while when she realized something important and stopped.

Wait... I don't know where Maiku is!

Maiku, who was busy looking for Karen, only realized that he had lost track of Miina when he was back near the karaoke contest stage. He thought Karen might be somewhere in the huge audience, and when he turned back to tell Miina they should split up and search, she was no longer there. He quickly looked around, but she was not anywhere nearby. He called out her name, but got no response. She was actually gone.

Damnit! Maiku cursed to himself, standing in the middle of the crowd. *What the hell is going on?*

It was as if there was a curse on the three of them keeping them apart. They were separated, found each other, one ran off... If this was the work of the goddess of destiny, then she certainly liked practical jokes.

Maiku was done feeling annoyed by his helpless situation, now he was mad. To make matters worse, there was an untalented fool singing from the stage. When he was done the MC came out in his flashy get-up.

"All right ladies and gentlemen, it's time to pick a volunteer from the audience again! Who among you has confidence in their skills?"

Before the MC was even finished speaking, Maiku, not even sure of what he was doing, raised his hand.

"You look ready to go, young man! Come on up to the stage!" the MC invited. Maiku, who was standing on the outside of the viewing area, wove through the audience and climbed up to the front of the stage. He was not even sure exactly what he was planning to do yet. But when the MC handed him the microphone he suddenly had a plan to go with his strange impulse to get on the stage.

"So, what are you going to sing for us?"

Maiku ignored the MC's question, took a deep breath and yelled into the microphone.

"Miiinaaa! Kareeeen!" His scream, amplified by the speakers, carried well past the audience. Maiku continued to scream, unaffected by the taken aback audience. "I'm up here! Maiku Kamishiro is up here!"

People walking by stopped at the sound of Maiku's desperate screams. Sure enough, his screams managed to reach the ears of Miina and Karen who both happened to be in the vicinity.

"Maiku?"

"Maiku?"

They were in different places, but his voice reached them at exactly the same time. They both went running through the audience to the stage. They climbed up to where Maiku was standing with the microphone and ran at him from both sides.

"Maiku!"

"Maiku!"

Maiku fell backwards, unable to stand up against their enthusiasm.

"Maikuu!" said Miina, burying her face in his shirt.

"We finally are back together!" Karen said, clinging to him tightly.

The audience was stunned for a while by the unexpected reunion scene they were witnessing. Then a few people started applauding, and the applause spread quickly over the crowd like a tsunami. Enveloped in the warm applause from the audience, Maiku, for some reason, felt like he was going to cry.

"What?! Maiku gave you that cat stuffed animal?" Karen's voice echoed through the bathroom as she jumped up out of the water in her excitement. As a result, Miina was now staring right at Karen's body.

"Uh, yeah," Miina said, turning away.

"You're so lucky! That's not fair!" whined Karen.

After they got home from the festival Miina and Karen got in the bath together, and Miina told her love alliance partner about getting the stuffed animal from Maiku.

"It seems like only you getting a present is somehow against the love alliance codes."

"That's why I'm reporting it to you!"

"Oh yeah…" Karen looked like she still did not quite understand, but she sunk back into the bathtub.

"When you were alone with Maiku, didn't he buy you anything?" Miina asked.

"Oh yeah! He bought me cotton candy!" Karen said after thinking about it for a minute.

"See, you got something from him, too!" Miina, who was feeling a little guilty about getting something from Maiku, looked relieved.

"But you get more points for getting a stuffed animal! Plus, I dropped my cotton candy before I had even finished it."

That was such a waste…

Karen suddenly imagined the half-eaten cotton candy lying on the ground, but it was a little late to be worrying about it now. But it was not just cotton candy. Despite the fact that he got it to try to distract her, Maiku did buy it for her. She felt stupid for dropping something so special. As she was regretting dropping the cotton candy, she remembered all of the events from when Maiku first bought it.

Maiku bought the cotton candy… he bit off one mouthful… then another... then he handed it to me... then I bit off a mouthful...

In her mind she pictured Maiku biting off some cotton candy and then herself doing the same thing. As if comparing fingerprints, she laid the two images of the cotton candy on top of one another in her mind. She realized that she and Maiku had eaten from the same part.

That was... an indirect kiss?

She realized this long after the fact and yet her face turned bright red and she felt dizzy. Miina might have been suspicious if they had not been in the hot bath.

I should report this to Miina...

As Karen opened her mouth to speak, Miina stood up and stepped out of the bathtub.

"I'm done, you can have it to yourself now."

"Um, Miina?"

"What?" Miina turned back as she opened the bathroom door.

I should report this... otherwise I would be breaking the codes!

Karen kept telling herself that, but she could not bring herself to report her indirect kiss with Maiku to Miina. She knew it was against the love alliance codes, but she wanted to keep this as her secret.

"What's wrong?" Miina asked, looking at Karen suspiciously. After all, it was Karen who had stopped her. Karen looked away from Miina and looked down at the bath water.

"N- nothing. Never mind," she said quietly.

Chapter 10: A Happy Melody

"Hey, what're you doing?"

Maiku looked at Miina with a confused expression on his face. The second he walked out of the school building she had grabbed his arm as if that was the natural thing to do.

"It's so we don't get separated! We don't want to have another incident like at the festival," said Miina.

"This way we don't have to worry about it," Karen said, grabbing his other arm, not wanting to be outdone by Miina.

"How would we possibly get separated on the way home from school?" Maiku asked, furrowing his brow.

"It could happen," Miina said, ignoring Maiku's annoyed expression.

"No it couldn't!" Maiku said firmly, trying to wriggle free of their hold, but they tightened their grip on both of his arms to show that they would not be letting go.

"Hey, cut it out!"

"Come on, it's just until we get home."

"Yeah!"

The three of them continued to bicker as they walked the short distance from the school building to the front gates. As they got to the gate, a man and a girl walked through and onto the school grounds. The man looked like he was in his mid forties and had no tie on. He was of a medium build and height and wore a jacket of a sober tone that was very becoming on him. He seemed very quiet. The girl who was walking a half-step behind him looked about Miina's age, and was wearing a summer dress that was so white one would hesitate even to touch it in fear of making a mark. The corners of her eyes seemed to turn down a little, adding a strong impression to her face that seemed almost too perfect. Her wavy hair hung down just past her shoulders and her bangs were held back by a headband, showing off her shiny forehead.

"Come on, just let go!" Maiku said, just as they passed the two people. As he twisted away from the girls, Karen lost her balance.

"Ahh!" Karen and the girl said in unison as Karen fell back onto her shoulder. Karen quickly turned around.

"I'm sor..." she started to apologize, but stopped when she saw the girl's face. The girl in the summer dress gulped when she saw Karen. After a few brief moments of staring at each other the girl spoke.

"Is that you, Onodera?" she asked as an incredulous expression crossed her face. These words made Karen come to her senses and she hid behind Maiku, avoiding the girl's eyes.

"It is you, isn't it? What are you doing here? And why did you disappear like that?" The girl asked, practically grabbing at Karen as she closed in on her. Karen looked petrified. Maiku, who was standing between the two girls, looked back at Karen.

"Do you know this girl?"

Karen's expression was frozen on her face and she gave no answer.

"Who are you?" the girl asked, finally noticing Maiku. She stared at him severely.

"I'm..." Maiku hesitated, "I'm a relative of Karen Onodera."

"Relative?" the girl said, raising one eyebrow inquisitively.

"What's the matter, Yukiko?" the man, who had already walked to the school building, called out to her. He had a calm voice that matched his appearance.

"Nothing, sir," the girl called Yukiko responded in a smooth voice. After taking one last look at Karen she ran off to join the man.

"Hey, Karen…" Maiku said that evening after they had finished dinner. He set down his tea cup on the table with all the now empty dishes. "Do you know that girl we saw on the way home?"

Karen, who was still eating slowly, looked tense.

"If you don't want to talk about it, I won't make you, but I'd appreciate it if you would."

After thinking for a while, Karen set her chopsticks down across her almost empty bowl of miso soup. Miina, who was sitting across the table from her, stopped stacking up the empty dishes.

"Her name is Yukiko Kachofugetsuin… and I do know her."

"Wait a minute… Kachofugetsudo, isn't that…?" Maiku interrupted.

"It's Kachofugetsuin," Karen corrected him.

"Oh, OK. Anyway, isn't she the girl who's going to do the opening performance at the piano concert? She's supposed to be the favorite pupil of the performer Mr. Nishi, who was a student at our school."

Maiku, who had recently been on the piano concert planning committee, remembered reading a long name in the plans.

"Really?" Apparently Karen had not yet heard that Yukiko would be playing at Seizo Nishi's piano concert. "So that's why she was at the school today?"

"Probably. I bet they came to check out the location. Oh yeah, I heard that tomorrow afternoon they're bringing their favorite piano to the auditorium. Apparently it's a really good one."

The piano concert was the day after tomorrow, Sunday. The plan was that Seizo Nishi was going to bring in his favorite fine piano to the auditorium where he would be performing.

"So that man who was with her was that pianist, whatizname?" Miina asked.

"Yeah, probably. That Setsugetsukain girl called him 'sir' so he must be her teacher."

"It's Kachofugetsuin," Karen dutifully corrected him.

"So how do you and that Hooinfugetsuko girl know each other, Karen?"

"It's Kachofugetsudo," Karen said, meaning to correct Miina.

"Don't you mean Kachofugetsuin?" said Maiku.

"Oh, yeah."

After that foolish exchange, Karen reluctantly told them about her and Yukiko.

Yukiko Kachofugetsuin had been one of Karen's classmates. They went to a famous girls' school that was known as a school for elite girls in the area. It was famous for its arts and music program and many now-famous musicians and artists had attended it. The tuition was outrageous so all the girls there were from very well-to-do families. The reason Karen, an orphan, was able to go there was because she was an incredibly gifted pianist.

Karen discovered her skill by playing on the electronic keyboard the children's home had in its play area. At first Karen just randomly hit

143

the keys, but when one of the workers gave her a little instruction, she was soon able to play simple songs. Karen, who was very withdrawn and did not have any friends at the home, began playing the electronic keyboard every day, and she soon showed remarkable improvement.

When she started elementary school and had the chance to use the school's piano she became increasingly devoted to music. She spent her lunch period and long hours after school playing the piano, and when she went back to the home she let her fingers glide over the keys of the electronic keyboard, longing for the clear tones of the piano.

By third grade she could play most songs after just seeing the music once. Her talent caught the eye of a music teacher who volunteered to give her private lessons. It was with that teacher that she first experienced formal piano instruction much beyond the level of the music classes in school. But in less than one year of studying with that teacher, she reached the point where there was no more he could teach her.

In sixth grade, she was encouraged to take a private middle and high school candidacy test because she had such high potential to succeed at a music college in the future. She passed. She received top scores on both the interview and skills sections of the exam. She was accepted as a special student in the music department of the school and all her expenses were waived.

It was a dream come true for Karen. Of course she was excited for the opportunity to be in an environment in which she could play her beloved piano, but more than that, she was happy to be able to leave the children's home. She was very thankful that they had taken her in when she had had no one else, but life there had never been fun. That was because Karen was an indecisive, dawdling cry baby, so the workers treated her like a troublesome child. Though she was young, she knew that it was her own fault whenever the workers yelled at her and she never felt like she fit in there. When Karen moved into the school dormitories she felt, for the first time in her life, that she belonged somewhere. This was her own place. She had paid to be there with her piano skills. It was the first place where she could be herself and not feel inferior.

Even in music classes among the other students with recognized musical skills who had passed the rigorous exams, Karen excelled. The only other student who matched Karen's skill level was Yukiko Kachofugetsuin. As the daughter of the president of a successful company, her childhood was completely different from Karen's. If Karen had not been chosen as a special student for the music department, surely the two would never have met.

When Karen realized that her "place of her own" was only secure so long as she proved that she really had the skills they thought she did, her attitude toward practicing completely changed. Before she had played piano for her own enjoyment, but now it was the only means she had to protect her little piece of heaven. Of course she would not be sent away because of a small drop in performance evaluations, as long as she was not acting up. But it was different for her as a special student on full scholarship than it was for the children whose parents were paying. Whether she did well in other subjects or not, she at least had to be near the top in her piano playing skills. She had to make it clear that she was better than the other students and there was no reason for them not to keep her on as a full-scholarship student. She had to make them think she was special. Otherwise she would feel like she was living in a community where she owed everybody something. That would be like she was back in the children's home with everyone thinking of her as a burden.

Perhaps because of the trauma of being raised in a home and treated insensitively, Karen had a complex about being troublesome to others. Yukiko seemed like a threat to the life she had worked so hard to achieve. It was not as if they competed directly with each other, but Karen could not help but find Yukiko very disagreeable. Yukiko, coming from a rich family, had been given formal piano instruction from when she was very young and had been blessed with a much more encouraging environment than an orphan like Karen. Yukiko had wonderful parents, lived in a large house, had beautiful clothes, and yet she still had the greed to try to be the top of the music class. She knew that her resentment was unjustified, but she could not do away with her negative feelings toward Yukiko.

During the three years Karen spent at the middle school she put all of her energy into improving her piano skills. Her enthusiasm toward playing piano was such a contrast to her apathy toward other classes that it seemed very bizarre to the other students. This made Karen, who had never really fit in with the other students, even more of a loner. However, she was rewarded for her efforts and excellent piano performance by being welcomed to the high school as a special student.

Everything seemed to be going well during cherry blossom season when Karen started classes at the high school. However, one month later a small accident threw the gears of destiny off their course. It happened one rainy day. Karen slipped and fell down the school stairs. Fortunately, it was not an emergency, but she fell on her arm and hurt her right hand. It turned out that she had only sprained her wrist, but the tendon of her pinky finger was severely damaged. The doctors immediately operated on it and within a few weeks she was able to manage everyday activities without any problem, but she never regained complete use of her right pinky. For someone who wanted to be a pianist, that was a death certificate for her future. She would never again be able to play piano like she did before. This fact threatened all hope she had for the future.

Unfortunately, her dismay was intensified by the news of an upcoming piano competition for high school students. This particular competition was regarded so highly that performing well there paved the way to becoming a respected pianist. Naturally, Karen had been practicing vigorously every day and putting more into her preparation than any other student. When she learned that her finger was never going to completely heal, she felt everything she had worked for collapse around her in a second. She closed herself in her dormitory room and hardly ate for days.

Why did she have to slip and fall? Why did she fall in a way that would hurt her hands that were as important as her life? It would have been better to hit her head and get amnesia. It would have even been better to have broken her neck and died than not be able to play the piano anymore…

There was a rumor that when a scholarship student in the sports department had been injured and could no longer play, she had to withdraw from the school. If that were true, would Karen, too, have to leave the school now that she could no longer play the piano like before? If that happened, it would be back to the children's home for her. Even if she were allowed to stay, she would no longer be a promising student, but a burden, only kept on so the school could keep up their reputation. It sickened her to imagine herself smiling calmly at the other music students as they avoided looking at her. She especially wondered what her rival Yukiko would think when she saw her awkward position.

She could not take it anymore. She did not want to be treated as a burden; she did not want to be looked down upon with cold stares from the other students.

She could not bear to go back to the pathetic place she had escaped from by the power of her own ten fingers on a keyboard. She thought long and hard and made her decision a few days before the piano competition. She packed up the food that had been left outside her door, took it and her few possessions in an old trunk and snuck out of the dormitory.

Karen went to the nearest station, got on the night train and headed for the house that was in the picture she had had with her when she was found. She knew that there was little chance anything would come of her going there. But all she could think of was escaping from the horrible reality in which she was living.

Karen knew the location of the lake where a UFO had been sighted years before. After all the news coverage she had looked at the library's newspaper archive to read about it. She also remembered that when the house from her picture had been on the news the reporter had said, "That's all from West Ocean Gate in lakeside Kizaki." Relying on this information, Karen went in search of her home, got lost, and finally met Maiku.

Maiku and Karen did not know what to say after Karen's long story about her past. Finally, Miina broke the silence.

"You've been through so much…" Miina managed to say.

"Yes, I've been through a lot," Karen said, looking down at the small scar on the joint of her right pinky finger. A light bulb went on in Maiku's head.

"Is the reason you're so clumsy because you hurt your hand, Karen?"

"No, I've always been a bit out of it."

"Oh…" With that short exchange the mood lightened.

"Let's forget about the past," said Miina, standing up, as if to finalize it.

"Yeah," Maiku said, nodding at Miina who started clearing the table. Then he turned to Karen and said, "Now you belong here."

"Yeah. Just forget about all the bad stuff that has happened!" Miina said as she took the dishes out to the kitchen. Karen watched her go with an expression of mixed emotion on her face.

"Hey, you there!"

The next day Maiku, as one of the only members of the piano concert planning committee, was running around making sure things were running smoothly at the school, when he was stopped as he walked by the auditorium. He turned to look and saw Yukiko standing at the door. She had come with her private instructor, Seizo Nishi, who had come to oversee the delivery of his fine piano. Today, quite in contrast to the white dress she wore yesterday, she was wearing a bright red dress. It might have been the dress for the nest day's performance, considering they were having a dress rehearsal later that day.

"You're related to Onodera, right?"

"Yes…"

"I was wondering if you would do me a favor."

"Sure, if I can."

"I want you to give this to Onodera," she said, pulling an envelope out of her music and handing it to Maiku.

It was a long white envelope made of very high quality paper and on the front was written "To Ms. Karen Onodera" in a practiced hand that matched her appearance. It seemed that a lot of time and consideration had been put into this letter. Maiku took the envelope and turned it over in his hands. In the lower corner of the back she had written in small words, almost inconspicuous "From Yukiko Kachofugetsuin."

"I'll give it to her, but she has work this afternoon so she's already gone home."

"Oh, I see," Yukiko said looking confused. "When will she be back?"

"Probably not until the evening. I'm not going home until around then either."

"Well that won't do," Yukiko muttered to herself in annoyance. Having been raised as a spoiled rich girl, she was used to having everything her way.

"You can't wait that long?" Maiku asked curtly. It seemed that Yukiko's annoyance was contagious. Yukiko spoke politely, but she still managed to make everything sound like an order, and that provoked Maiku. He felt like he understood why Karen did not have fond memories of Yukiko.

"No, that's fine. Just make sure you give it to her today, as soon as possible."

Maiku nodded silently and put the envelope in his uniform pocket.

"Thanks. Bye," Yukiko thanked him, and headed back into the auditorium.

"Here, Karen." Maiku delivered the envelope from Yukiko just as the sun was setting on the long summer's day. Karen and Miina had just gotten back from work. Karen stiffened when she saw Yukiko's name written on the back of the envelope. She ripped open the envelope, still standing in the foyer, and as she read the letter her expression became more and more tense.

"What's it say?" Maiku asked, holding back the urge to read over her shoulder.

"It says to meet her at the school auditorium tonight at 10:00pm," Karen read aloud in a small voice.

"10pm? The school gates will be locked already," Maiku said with a confused expression on his face.

"'Please come in the private entrance, I'll be sure to leave it unlocked,' it says."

"Oh. But why would she ask you to meet her at the school so late?"

"She probably wants to settle things."

"Settle what?"

"Our piano skills."

"Your skills?"

"Yes, I told you yesterday that I ran away the day before the piano competition. Before that Yukiko and I had been competing to see which of us was the more skilled pianist. We never really said it, but we both thought of the competition as a way to settle the question."

"And so... uh, what was her name again?"

"Kachofugetsuin."

"Yeah, that Kachofugetsudou girl wants to settle things now that she's found you?"

"So that's a letter of challenge then?" asked Miina who had been silently listening to the conversation. Her choice of words was quite old-fashioned.

"Well, uh... I guess so."

"Then we'll have to have tonkatsu (pork cutlet) for dinner!"

"Why?" Maiku looked at her as if to say, "What the hell are you talking about?" Miina looked at him as if to say, "Isn't it obvious?"

"It's a hearty meal, it will help her win!"

"Miina," Maiku started to say something to her, but she turned her back on him and started to put her shoes back on.

"I'm gonna go get meat at the store. If I run I should make it back in time."

"Wait a minute," Maiku said, grabbing Miina's shoulder as she was about to run out the door. "Challenge or no challenge, with her injury..." Maiku hesitated, not wanting to say it in front of Karen.

"She can't play like before," Miina said for him. "So you're saying she won't have a chance?"

"Well, yeah..."

"That's so stupid!"

"What?"

"Because it's not true. It doesn't matter if she wins or loses. That's not important anymore. She belongs here, so no matter what happens Karen can come back here. Right?"

"Yeah… that's right," Maiku looked like he had been caught off guard.

"So she just has to try so that whatever-her-name-is can feel satisfied. Right, Karen?"

"Ye- yes," Karen quickly answered, surprised to be back in the conversation.

"So I'm going to the store and…"

"Wait a minute!" Maiku stopped her again just as she was about to leave.

"What? What is it this time?" Miina said turning around crossly.

"If it doesn't matter whether she wins or loses, we don't really need to bother with the hearty meal."

"Oh yeah." Miina finally realized that her actions were contradicting her words. But it seemed like she was set on having tonkatsu for dinner. "Well, whatever. It can't do any harm," she said trying to justify it as she ran out the door.

"It's getting pretty close to time," Maiku said, looking at Miina to see how she was. He had been looking at the clock non-stop since nine o'clock. Maiku usually went up to his room after dinner, but today he was so worried about Karen that he stayed in the sitting room watching a television show that did not particularly interest him and sipping lukewarm tea. Miina had found the television set at the dumpster and brought it home. Instead of a TV table, it was sitting on top of a cardboard orange box. It made them look very poor.

"Yes," Karen said, setting her tea cup on the table as she stood up. She felt butterflies in her stomach and put her hand on her abdomen. Miina, who was sitting with her legs stretched out in front of the television looked up and noticed.

"Does your stomach hurt?"

"No, it doesn't really hurt, it's just…"

"I did buy pretty big cutlets, maybe it was too much."

"No, I didn't overeat, I'm just nervous."

"Really? That's surprising," Miina said with her eyes wide in mock surprise.

"I get nervous sometimes too, you know," Karen said, pouting.

"Just sometimes?"

"Miina!"

"If you keep dawdling you'll be late!" Miina said, hurrying along Karen who was puffing out her cheeks.

"Oh yeah!" Karen was so nervous she could no longer tell whether Miina was making fun of her or not. She started heading out into the hall.

"Oh, Karen?"

"What is it, Maiku?" Karen asked, turning back to Maiku.

"Will you, uh, be OK without us?" he asked, looking concerned.

"I'm not going! There's something I want to see on TV," Miina said, without even looking up.

"Miina…" Maiku started to say something to Miina, but Karen interrupted him.

"I'll be fine by myself."

"But it's dark out, and…"

"She's just going to the school, it doesn't matter whether it's dark out or not," Miina said, sounding completely unconcerned.

"Yeah, but…" Maiku seemed as worried as a father sending his daughter out on her first errand alone. "Aren't you worried about her, Miina?"

"Not at all!" Miina looked at Maiku dubiously, "Why are you so worried anyway, Maiku?"

"Well, uh…"

Maiku hesitated at the direct question. Of course he was worried about her walking alone at night, being a girl and all, but that was only the surface. The real reason he was worried was something completely different, something he could not put into words. Yukiko was a girl who had appeared from Karen's past, a past he had known nothing about. He had a feeling that if Karen were in contact with Yukiko, she would be taken captive by the past she left behind. He felt like she would somehow be taken away from him.

"Um, I've really got to get going," Karen said hesitantly to Maiku who was sitting silently, unable to put his feelings into words.

"Oh, yeah, you wouldn't want to be late."

"Well, I'll see you guys later."

Maiku seemed strangely upset about it all, but Miina was calm and cool.

"See you when you get home," Miina said, as naturally as a mother would say to her child when she left for school in the morning.

At night the school was silent, as if the hustle and bustle of the day had never happened. The door to the private entrance was unlocked, just as Yukiko had written in the letter, and Karen entered the school grounds through it. Karen walked through the brush behind the school building, relying on the moonlight to guide her, and made her way to the auditorium where they were to meet. There was something strange about the empty school, and if someone had suddenly spoken she would surely have fallen down in surprise.

Maybe I should have had Maiku come with me...

Karen started to lose her nerve as she walked to the auditorium. She pushed the heavy door open. It was dim inside and the moonlight shining through the windows bathed the stage around the piano in a white blue light.

"So you came." Karen almost jumped in surprise when Yukiko suddenly spoke as she approached the stage. Yukiko walked out from the side of the stage and stood by the piano. "Long time no see, Onodera."

"Yukiko..." Karen, who was now at the base of the stage, looked up at Yukiko's face that was as fixed as a doll's.

"I won that piano competition," Yukiko said suddenly, confusing Karen. She did not know whether she should congratulate her or not. "But winning the competition without you there wasn't worth anything," Yukiko spit out. So Karen was right about the reason Yukiko had called her tonight.

"You know why I called you here, don't you, Onodera?" Karen nodded silently in response and Yukiko sat down at the piano and opened the lid. "Good." She pulled the cloth that was covering the keys and said, "You don't mind if I go first, of course."

Yukiko set her hands on top of the keys and just as she was about to begin playing, Karen raised her voice.

"Wait! Yukiko, I don't even play piano now..."

"I don't want to hear your whining!" Yukiko yelled out, and began playing before Karen could respond.

"Yukiko…"

The moment the first sound rang through the air, Karen drew in a breath at the exquisitely sharp sound. When she looked closely it looked as if the ten long, thin fingers were dancing beautifully across the keys, spinning out a skein of gorgeous sounds. She immediately recognized the song as the one that was chosen for the competition.

Wow, Yukiko is even better than I remembered…

The constant practice made her able to carefully hit the perfect note and everything was perfect because of her incomparable precision. She hit the right keys without hesitation and without ever losing the tempo. She understood the motif of the song and used that to make the best phrases sound even more beautiful. Sometimes her fingers were flying so fast they tried to break away from the plan, but other than that she performed almost perfectly. It was understandable that she had won the competition.

Karen was so swept away by the beautiful melody Yukiko had played, that she felt rooted to the floor. She finally let out the breath she had drawn when the unearthly song was over. She had sweat on her forehead. After the reverberation from the last note had finally dissolved into the pale blue moonlight, she felt a dark reminder in her mind.

There's no way I can do this.

It is said to take three days of practice to recover from one day of missed piano practice. Karen had not even touched a piano, much less practiced, in over two months. Even if she had not hurt her finger, if she had stayed at the school and kept practicing, she was not sure that she would have been able to perform better than Yukiko just had.

Yukiko got up from the seat and walked down to Karen's side. "It's your turn."

Karen stood firm in place with her head hanging down. Yukiko gave her a cold stare and said, "What's wrong? You came this far and now you're just gonna run away again?"

Karen made tight fists with her two hands that were hanging by her sides. She lifted up her head and walked steadily to the stage, ignoring Yukiko's stare. She sat down in front of the piano and looked at the keys. She thought she would never touch the orderly spread of keys on a piano again. She took a deep breath and lightly set her fingers on them, as if she was afraid to make a noise. The keys felt cold, perhaps because of the moonlight. Karen could feel Yukiko staring intently at her from in front of the stage. She hit a key, as if testing out the piano. It had a good sound. It was obvious that this piano was not like the ones in a school classroom.

She had come this far, there was no turning back. Karen prepared herself and begun to play. Her hands remembered the competition song without needing her eyes to read the music. At first she played slowly, feeling around for the keys. Then she gradually raised the tempo and produced a complicated and beautiful melody. The notes worked together to form a full resonance. The powerful rhythms made the sounds swell, pulling in anyone who heard. Even as she played the flourishing melody, inside she was tortured by nervousness and impatience. She was cursed by the after effects of her injury and her lack of practice. Her fingers would not do what she told them to.

It's no good. I can't bring out the quality of the song or the piano.

The more she played the more those thoughts clouded her mind and she began to feel like this fine piano was blaming her for not being able to satisfactorily exhibit its full greatness. She felt full of sadness and regret and felt as if she were going to cry.

This isn't good enough... I can't...

The feelings swelled up inside her and she lost control of her fingers. She quickly tried to recover, but her mind went blank. At that very moment Miina's words popped into her head.

(It doesn't matter if she wins or loses. That's not important now.)

"Huh?"

Karen felt a strong wind blow through her mind and sweep away the depressing pauses in her playing.

(She belongs here, so no matter what happens, Karen can come back here. Right?)

Yeah... that's right. I belong somewhere now.

The second she remembered that she felt relieved. Why had she been so desperate? She did not need to play the piano to protect her own haven anymore.

There was no reason to keep torturing her right pinky finger that did not move quite right. She did not have to play for others; she could play how she wanted to. She could play calmly and enjoy it.

The melody of Karen's playing changed to reflect her change of heart. The resonance became lighter, as if it had been released from some heavy force. To put it nicely, she played freely; to put it badly, she played in a loose, coarse manner. A questioning look appeared on Yukiko's face as she watched Karen intently. But Karen was soon unaware of Yukiko's presence as she started playing only for herself.

This is fun, thought Karen from the bottom of her heart. How long had it been since she had played piano feeling like this? It might have been since she played newly learned songs over and over in the elementary school classroom after school.

She did not have to think about anything. She just let her fingers glide over the keys and produce joyous sounds. After she played the last note of the song, her mind was filled with a mysteriously uplifting feeling. However, Yukiko's firm voice put a damper on that feeling.

"That definitely was not good enough to beat me."

It was certainly true that her performance would not have received much praise by the competition judges' standards. Karen knew that herself and there was nothing for her to say.

"But that was still a wonderful performance."

What?

Karen thought she had not heard correctly. Yukiko climbed up to the stage and stood next to Karen who was looking at her blankly.

"You're happy now, aren't you, Onodera?"

Karen, still not quite following, nodded.

"I thought so, otherwise there's no way you could play like that." Yukiko's expression had softened. "I was actually planning to take you back today."

"Take me back?"

"Yes. If you seemed to be in a bad spot I was going to ask my father if we could take you in at our house."

Karen had never imagined anything like this. She had no idea why Yukiko would be so kind to her.

"But why?"

"Why? Because we're friends. I couldn't ignore a friend in need."

"Yukiko…"

Karen was so choked up that she could not manage to say any-thing else. She and Yukiko had been in the same music department, in the same classes since Middle school. But, perhaps because she thought of her as a rival, she never really considered her a friend. She even thought of her as a nasty person who was threatening the place she could finally call her own. But despite all that, Yukiko considered Karen a friend. She probably also felt competitive with Karen because they both held the same goals. But despite that, or maybe even because of that, she felt a sense of friendship toward Karen. Karen finally realized that she was lim-iting her place to belong by closing her heart off to others.

"I wanted to talk to you about this long before, but I thought it might upset you, so I was hesitant to say anything."

If Yukiko took in Karen who had left the dorms, it would mean that Karen had to give up her spot as a full-scholarship special student in the music department. That would mean that her future as a pianist was over, and although Yukiko meant nothing but kindness by it, to Karen it would sound like the cruelest possible sentence. It was completely under-standable that Yukiko would hesitate to bring such a thing up, especially considering that Karen had the wrong idea about her and her motives. She had every reason to doubt whether Karen, in the mental state she had been in, would be able to accept such a proposition.

"I hesitated for too long and then, you know…"

Karen knew exactly what she meant. Karen had quietly snuck

out of the dormitory before Yukiko had a chance to say anything.

"I felt so bad. I didn't even realize just how upset you were even though you were my friend. I'm so sorry."

I'm the one who should be apologizing...

Karen opened her mouth to apologize, but instead she just started sobbing.

"Uh, what's wrong? Did I say something I shouldn't have?" Yukiko looked really upset about Karen who suddenly started crying.

"No, no, it's nothing you said. I'm just so happy. I'm so happy that you thought of me like that..."

"Don't surprise me by crying so much all of a sudden like that!"

Karen was still sitting on the chair in front of the piano sobbing. Yukiko handed her a perfectly folded white handkerchief.

"Here, dry your tears. You're happy now, aren't you? You don't have to cry like this."

"Y-yeah. You're right," Karen managed while wiping her tears with the handkerchief.

"Onodera?" Yukiko seemed a little uncomfortable as she put the handkerchief back in her pocket. "You really don't want to come live with my family? I really don't mind at all. Actually, I'd be really happy if you came."

"I'm sorry, I'm really happy that you want me to come, but..." Karen spoke flatly to Yukiko whose cheeks were flushed. "I have a home to go back to now."

"What, do you have to go to the bathroom again?" Miina, who was watching television in the sitting room, turned to look at Maiku who had come downstairs.

"No, I'm thirsty so I thought I'd get a glass of barley tea."

"Yeah, right. You're just worried about Karen so you can't get any work done." Miina had hit the nail right on the head and Maiku paused for a minute.

"That's not it at all…"

"Oh come on. Before, you said you had to go to the bathroom, and now you're back again. You've come downstairs once about every ten minutes! It's so obvious."

"I can't help it if I'm worried," Maiku said defiantly, when he realized Miina had him.

"Hmm, you sure seem to worry about Karen."

"Of course, she's like family."

"All right then, if it were me instead of Karen in a similar situation, would you be this worried?"

"Uh…" Maiku hesitated at the unexpected question. "Oh… of course."

"Then why did you pause?"

"Uh… no reason," Maiku said, taking a half step back as Miina started to get up. Then he heard the unlocked door open from the outside. "She's back!" Maiku proclaimed and ran to the front door.

Karen was standing halfway in the door and was surprised to see Maiku come to meet her so energetically.

"I'm home," She said cheerfully, happy to be able to say those words and mean them.

"Welcome home," said Miina, smiling sweetly from behind Maiku.

Chapter 11: A Pair and One

"I'm home!"

Sunday afternoon, Miina came back from shopping, put the food in the refrigerator, stepped into the living room and said, "Karen, I picked up something good while I was out shopping." Karen was slumped over the low table, breathing peacefully with her cheek resting on her open notebooks.

"Oh, she's asleep."

Karen had turned down Miina's invitation to go shopping, saying she would study, but at this rate, she could not hope for good marks on their rapidly approaching midterm exams. Miina watched her sleep, and she must have been dreaming about buying clothes in a boutique, because she said, "I can't pick! I want all the clothes here!"

Miina sighed at this foolish sleep-talk.

She's so carefree.

Karen looked so comfortable that Miina would have felt bad to wake her, and instead put on her sandals by the veranda and went outside. She walked around to the front yard, past the clothes lines where drying laundry fluttered in the cool breeze, and came out near the front entrance. A dirty inflatable pool with its air let out was there. It was the "something good" she had picked up at the dump, left there as oversized garbage. It looked like it had been stored in a shed for a long time and was very dirty, but, from what she could see, it did not have any holes in it. To check this, she picked up the vinyl pool and carried inside the house. She cleaned it in the bathtub, dried it with a cloth, and carried it back outside. She used a tube to inflate the round pool, but this was more difficult than she had imagined. Most of it would not inflate and her bulging cheeks were hurting. Just like her chest, it seemed it would not expand very easily. She kept with it though, and after a while it had expanded into a round pool-like shape.

This looks good.

Miina breathed a sigh of relief and set the pool in the front yard.

Karen would be so surprised when she woke up.

For the two girls, and perhaps Maiku as well, the pool in front of their house would be a special sight. That is because it would remind them of the summer day in the picture that had first drawn them to this house.

They must have played in the water in front of the house on nice days like this.

Standing a bit away, looking at the pool with the house in the background, Miina, who was immersed in creating false nostalgia from memories that did not exist, was caught in a feeling that something was not right.

'Something isn't right,' she thought, but she had changed both the position of the pool and her own position many times, and still never managed to capture the scene of the photo.

Weird...

After trying every possibility, she decided to get the photograph to use as a model. There was no need to recreate it so exactly, but it had become a matter of pride for her. She also wanted to surprise Karen and Maiku by reproducing the scene as closely as possible. Miina went into the house to her room on the second floor, grabbed the photo, and compared it to the scene she had created.

What? Could it be that...

Whatever she had realized made Miina's face stiffen suddenly. She ran up the unpaved hilly road and came out on the street along the lake's rocky shore. Comparing the view with the photograph in her hand, she stepped back until she had crossed the road and she backed into a hill built of large concrete blocks.

"This isn't it."

Miina found the entrance to the hilly road on her right and ran toward it. She climbed the weedy hill and stopped at the top of the slope. Looking at her house, she took a few steps down.

"Here."

Miina stopped where the house looked the same as it did in the photo. The picture was definitely taken from here. And the vinyl pool would be...

She looked down at the pool.

"But this is..."

When she realized too late that the place she was looking at was divided by a street from the house they shared, she was struck with intense dizziness.

"No way... that's.... Why...?"

Where Miina now stood was somewhat higher than the road, while the house they lived in was a step lower than the road. So, looking down from where they thought the picture had been taken, the angle made it so the rocky lake path hardly appeared in her field of vision. Because of this, in the picture, it looked like their house was right behind the pool.

But in reality, a large asphalt snake stretched between them.

"Then that means... the house, the kids in the photo lived in was..."

Understanding what the heroine of a horror movie must feel, waiting for the terror that would cause her entire body to freeze, but compelled by some incomprehensible force to keep walking through the darkness, Miina turned around slowly. There stood a two-story house much like the one they now occupied. No, it would be more accurate to call it 'something that had once been a house.' It looked like it had not been repaired in years, the paint was peeling, and there was rust on the roof. The storm windows were shut and so dirty it was impossible to tell what color they were originally. Every part of it was worn down, and it looked like a strong member of the Judo team would be able to take the house down with one push. Naturally, it did not look like anyone lived there.

"This is the house we were born in..."

They still did not know which of the girls was related to Maiku, so it was not necessarily true that Miina had been born there. Miina was still recovering from the shock and did not think of this, but continued staring vacantly at the house. She was an abandoned child and for her, the house in the picture, though she had no memory of it, was a means of connecting herself with the family she knew must exist. That's why when she was hurt and had no where else to turn, she ran to this, 'the house she used to live in.' Even so, coming to the wrong house, even though it was so important, was so incredibly stupid, it could not even be made into a joke.

They found the house based on just one picture. There, Miina and Karen met and both were accepted by Maiku. One of them was Maiku's relative, and one was completely unrelated. An uncertain and unsteady relationship founded on a picture of a boy and a girl that the three of them each carried. She might be related to him. She might not be. She wanted to be related to him. She wanted to be unrelated. Which was related by blood? Was it Miina or Karen? With their feelings swinging like a pendulum, the three of them managed to live together under one roof. Under that roof, they had shared fun times, sad times, happy times, and difficult times. So much had happened. With every thing that happened, their feelings had grown closer, and their hearts had come together. Miina felt now as if she had spent her whole life living with Karen and Maiku in the house by the lake. Finding out that the house they had lived in together and believed was the house they were born in was, in fact, not this at all left Miina completely shattered. It was as if the house was telling her the two months they'd spent living as a family was nothing but a lie. The pathetic shape of the abandoned house told her mercilessly that the happy days she had just glimpsed in the picture would never return.

It wasn't true. She wanted to leave this place and forget everything. But even as she thought that, she found herself drawn to the old house like a moth to a flame. Moving closer, she saw the full extent of the damage. Weeds grew all around the entrance, and the glass in the door was mostly broken. She must have passed this house many times on the street, but this was the first time she had ever noticed it. Perhaps it was for that reason she thought of the house as something that had suddenly appeared out of her nightmares.

She had no intention of going inside, but with the mental state like one who knows she will see something frightening, she put her hand to the door, which slid open as if it could not wait another second for its long-awaited visitor. She did not know if the lock was broken, or if the door simply had not been locked. Miina stepped inside, as if beckoned by an unseen hand. The rusty smell of the stuffy house filled her nose. The stairs and the hallway they led to were covered in a thick layer of dust, and Miina could not bring herself to take off her shoes. Still in her sandals, she stepped up, but the weathered wood creaked in protest. She continued and the floor squeaked under her careful footsteps. The layout was not very different from the house they lived in. Sunshine leaked in through holes in the walls and ceiling and it was surprisingly bright inside. Without knowing what she was searching for, she looked around the first floor. The household goods that remained were dusty, and the table and closet in the Japanese-style room were open, for some reason. That caught her interest, and Miina went into that room, looking around her again. At first she thought a burglar might have broken in, but they did not seem they had been forced open. After a while, Miina realized she remembered having seen this scene before.

That was it. This was the same as before. When she ran away in the night with the parents who had raised her...

Now that she thought about it, the house had the atmosphere that its inhabitants had picked up only the objects closest to them, and fled. It looked likely that the owners of this house had some reason to hide and had left everything as it was. And at that time, their children, who would have slowed them down, were left behind, just like the rest of their things.

I shouldn't have come...

Shaking her head, to rid herself of unpleasant thoughts, Miina walked out of the Japanese-style room. She then noticed a photograph had fallen in front of the closet. The sliding door of the closet was wide open and it looked like the photograph had fallen there by some chance of fate. It must have fallen a long time ago, because there was so much dust piled on the photograph that she hesitated to pick it up.

Shock ran across her face the instant she spotted the photograph. Disbelieving, she picked it up, and brushed away the dust that obscured the picture with her hand. When she did, the image of the girl and boy playing in the vinyl pool appeared beneath it.

"This can't be..."

There was no need to compare it to the picture in her pocket she had brought from her own room. It was unmistakably the same as the picture she had had when she was abandoned. Miina was so shocked by the discovery of a fourth picture just like the one that she, Karen, and Maiku all carried that she dropped it. It fell face down, and as she reached down to pick it up she noticed something written on the back, and paused.

"Huh?"

At first she could not tell what it said. It was not that she could not read the words, but what was written there was so shocking that she did not immediately understand what it meant. She picked up the picture in her trembling hands and looked intently at the back, holding her breath. In black permanent marker it said, "Maiku and Karyn O.'s first time in the pool."

"This means that…"

Miina turned it over and stared at the front, her eyes wide. There was no doubt. The note on the back proved that this was a picture of Maiku and Karen when they were young.

"Oh. So it's Karen who's related to him."

She had never expected there questions to be answered in such a way. She had thought they would never find the answer to the mystery.

In fact she had started to think it did not matter whether they found out or not, but now the case was closed. It suddenly all seemed so pointless to Miina as she stood there.

She wondered how long she had been standing there. When she finally got a hold of herself, all sorts of thoughts were racing through her mind.

So Karen is Maiku's sister. That would make me completely unrelated to him. What will Maiku and Karen think when they find out? More importantly, how should I tell Karen?

There was so much to think about that she thought her head was going to explode. Miina took the picture and left the deserted house, as if she was trying to escape from it all. Her eyes had adjusted to the dimness of the house so that high noon sun seemed even brighter than usual. She walked to the street and crossed it without looking back. She started down the unpaved hill. When she arrived at the house she realized that she was still holding the picture with the evidence of who was really related to Maiku in her hand. She quickly shoved it into her pocket. She tried to breathe evenly again and pulled open the unlocked door. As soon as she walked into the house Karen came running out of the sitting room, as if she had been waiting for the sound of the door to signal Miina's return.

"You've gotta come see this, Miina!" Karen said, grabbing the startled Miina's hand and pulling her to the porch that looked onto the front yard. She pointed at the vinyl pool that was sitting next to the clothes line. "Look at that!"

Miina tried to say, "Oh, I brought that…" but Karen continued before she got a chance.

"I fell asleep while doing my homework and when I woke up it was there in the yard," Karen said with an excited look on her face.

I was wondering what the fuss was all about...

Miina felt relieved. Karen turned to her with a completely serious expression on her face and said, "Maybe it's a gift from Santa Claus!"

"What? You've got to be kidding," said Miina laughing at Karen's childish statement. "Santa Claus wouldn't come on such a hot day. We're not in Australia or anything."

"Then who?"

"I found it at the dumpster and brought it here."

"Really?" Karen looked at if she had been tricked when she learned the perfectly normal reason behind it. After she had calmed down a bit, she started to feel embarrassed about having sounded so serious about Santa Claus. She blushed. "Well, you know, it's kind of like, um… I was really surprised and um, I thought that maybe, um…"

Although what Karen said made no sense, Miina knew what she was trying to say. Miina knew that the vinyl pool had reminded Karen of the picture, just as it had for her. It was only natural that she was surprised to see that sitting in front of the house, just like in the picture. It was not that hard to believe that she would jump to the conclusion that it was a gift from above when she spotted it after just having woken up. Her nickname was Ms. Enigma, after all.

"Well, then should we change into swimsuits?"

"What?" Miina was caught off guard and she stared blankly at Karen. "Wait a minute, are you saying we should go in that pool?"

"Shouldn't we?"

"We're not kids, why would we play in a kiddie pool like that?"

"If you didn't plan to use it then why did you bring it here?"

Miina did not know how to respond. When she saw the pool at the dumpster all she had thought of was reenacting the scene in the picture and did not really consider anything else.

"You went to the trouble of bringing it; we might as well use it!"

Karen seemed like she really wanted to get in the pool. Miina, who was not interested, tried hard to think of a reason not to.

"It's much too small for the two of us!"

When they were children they may have been able to play together in a kiddie pool, but now that they were all grown up it would be a little tight, even if their chests were still as flat as when they were children. Karen tried to imagine her and Miina in the school uniforms squeezed into the small pool.

"I guess it would be a little tight," she said looking deep in thought.

"Yep," nodding, happy to have Karen agree with her.

"But it seems like such a waste not to use it after you brought it here," Karen said looking disappointed.

"If you really want to use it, why don't you go in alone? I won't try to stop you."

"It'd be so embarrassing alone, though!"

"Not as embarrassing as it would be if we both went in."

Maiku, who was coming downstairs to get some coffee, overheard them and peered around the corner at the two of them talking in the hall facing the front yard.

"What are you two doing?"

"Oh, Maiku," Karen pointed at the pool, "Look at that. Miina brought it."

Maiku looked where Karen was pointing and an expression of surprise ran across his face. The kiddie pool seemed to have a special meaning for him, too.

"Why did you bring that here?" Maiku said looking at Miina, but before she could answer Karen interrupted.

"We're gonna use it, of course."

"Seriously?" Maiku said turning to Miina with an expression that seemed to say, "No way."

"There's no way I'm getting in that pool," Miina said shaking her head.

"What!" Karen yelled in protest to Miina then turned to Maiku. "Do you want to go in the --"

"No way," Maiku answered before she had a chance to finish her question. "You've got to be kidding me."

"Come on, don't be like that! Let's go in the pool! If the two of us go in together it will be like in the picture."

"No it won't," Maiku said, curtly. "We don't even know whether it's you or not in that picture, anyway." Maiku's casual words seemed to make the air turn to ice.

"Ye…yeah, I guess you're right," Karen said, looking as disheartened as a cat that had been put in the bathtub. "We don't know if the girl in the picture is me or Miina."

"I didn't mean it like…" The three of them felt very awkward.

But I already know! The one in the picture…the one who is related to Maiku is Karen!

Those words caught in Miina's throat and she was unable to tell them. She needed more time to get her feelings together before she told them the truth.

"Oh yeah," Maiku said trying to break the silence. "I came down to get some coffee," he muttered unnecessarily and headed out to the dining room.

Miina followed Maiku out, but headed upstairs instead of going to the dining room. She went into the room she shared with Karen, and was overcome by exhaustion, having been released from the tense situation downstairs. She slumped down onto the tatami floor and took the picture she found at the deserted house out of her pocket. On the front were two very familiar children. But on the back were written words that would put an end to their temporary living arrangement.

What should I do?

Miina sighed as she looked down at the picture in her hands. She knew what she had to do. She had to show the picture to Maiku and Karen and tell them the truth. It even said in the love alliance codes she made with Karen that "if one of us finds out that she is related by blood to Maiku, she will immediately tell the other." She had just missed the perfect opportunity to tell them. She knew she could not keep it from them forever and had no intention of doing so. She knew that, but she still wanted more time. She wanted more time to deal with her feelings.

"Miina," Karen said suddenly, opening the door and looking in. Miina was so surprised she almost jumped up, and she quickly shoved the picture into a magazine that was near her.

"Wh- what is it?" Miina asked, looking tense.

"What do you want to do about the pool? I don't think we should just leave it out there."

"Ye- yeah, I guess not. Why don't we let the air out and bring it in?" Miina quickly stood up and walked out of the room pushing Karen with her, as if trying to keep her from going in. "We should do it right now, I'll help."

"Ugh, I finally finished it!" Karen said with a drawn and haggard face. She had been doing homework in the sitting room and walked into the kitchen as Miina was getting dinner ready. Since they lived in the same house, they decided it would be more efficient to have one person do the homework and the other just copy it. They divided up the subjects based on who was better at them. Miina was in charge of English and history, Karen modern and ancient Japanese. Neither of them was very good at math or science so they had given up on those subjects. Yesterday the ancient Japanese teacher assigned homework so Karen had been working on it since after lunch, except when she fell asleep for a little while.

"Good job," said Miina who was wearing an apron and turning the heat on under a pot full of water. "That sure took a while, didn't it?"

"There's always so much work for that class. I hate it."

"Are you sure it didn't take this long just because you fell asleep?"

Karen looked embarrassed. She turned to Miina who was taking a cleaver out from under the sink.

"So, what's for dinner tonight," Karen asked, trying to change the subject.

"The main dish will be pork miso soup with lots of shellfish. We'll have fried tofu and eggs cooked in soup and boiled spinach."

"What a Japanese meal!"

"I'm going to make a lot of the soup tonight, so we'll probably be eating it for several days. Hope you're ready for that."

"Go easy on me!"

Since they tried to keep things cheap at the Kamishiro house, they tended to make lots of things that would keep and then eat it for several days in a row. Miina started cutting up vegetables for the soup.

"Do you want me to help with anything," Karen asked.

"No, that's OK. I can do it myself," Miina said refusing Karen's help as if it was a crazy idea. People can improve over time. Miina had let Karen help in the kitchen many times, believing that with practice Karen would become a better cook, but Miina had given up on teaching her ever since the day she asked her to peel an onion and she ended up peeling each layer off until there was no more and there were tears streaming down her cheeks. She appreciated Karen's desire to help, but she had to turn her down if she wanted to make an edible meal for them.

"Oh, OK," Karen said looking disappointed.

"Oh yeah. If you've got nothing to do, why don't you clean our room?" Miina suggested, obviously trying to make Karen feel useful. Of course she actually just wanted Karen as far away from the kitchen as possible. But Karen was oblivious to all of that.

"Oh, sure," she said leaving the kitchen and climbing the stairs with light steps.

I thought I just cleaned upstairs recently...

She thought it was a little bit strange, but thought nothing of it as she headed into their room. Karen went to pick up the books and magazines off the floor before she vacuumed.

"What's this?" she said as she noticed a picture flutter out of the magazine she had just picked up. She stopped cleaning up to get the picture and noticed it was the familiar picture of two children playing in a pool. She wondered why such a special picture would be inside the magazine as she picked it up. She casually turned it over.

What...?

She looked at the words written on the back of the picture and her eyes widened. When she realized what she had just read she dropped all the books and magazines she had been holding.

"Maiku! Karen! Dinner's ready!" Miina yelled at he foot of the stairs. She soon heard the sound of doors sliding open. Miina went back to the kitchen and started bringing the food out to the sitting room where she saw Maiku who had just come down from his room.

"What's for dinner?"

"Pork miso soup, fried tofu and eggs, and boiled spinach," Miina said in one breath. "Where's Karen?"

"I dunno."

Usually Karen came running down the second she heard it was dinner time, Miina thought as she set the table. She laid out the plates and filled the bowls with rice, but Karen still had not come down by the time they were ready to eat. Miina took off her apron and went back to the stairs.

"Kaaareeen! Dinner!" she yelled, but there was no response from upstairs. "If you don't come soon we'll eat it all without you!"

Maybe she fell asleep again...

Miina went upstairs and opened the door to their room.

"Huh, she's not here."

She had assumed she would be there, but she was no where to

be seen. She walked into the room wondering where Karen could have gone and noticed the books and magazines scattered around the floor. Then her eyes fell on the picture next to them and she almost screamed.

"No... no... she didn't..."

Miina collapsed on the floor. Karen had seen the picture. She had seen the proof that she was related to Maiku. She had realized that she was not allowed to fall in love with Maiku.

What should I do? What should I do? What should I do?

Miina sat slumped down helplessly on the ground next to the magazines for a long while.

"Hey, what're you doing up there? Dinner's getting cold!" Maiku, who had gotten sick of waiting, came upstairs and looked into the room from the open door. Miina turned to look at him and the second she saw his face she burst into tears.

"Why didn't you tell us right away?!" he said in an angry voice after Miina explained what happened through her tears.

"I tried to tell you! I wanted to tell you, but..." Miina was still sitting slumped down on the floor. Maiku looked a little bit embarrassed as he looked down at Miina from where he was standing in the doorway. He seemed to realize that from Miina's position it was a little shocking to find out that she was not related to him so she had not been ready to tell them yet. He knew it would be cruel to blame her for any of this. What they needed to do was look for Karen. He realized something strange about that.

"Wait a minute, why would Karen leave?"

He could understand her leaving if she had found out that she was not related to him and felt like she no longer belonged here, but why would she leave after finding out that she was related to him? He could not understand.

"Maiku," said Miina, with her eyes brimming with tears, looking up at Maiku. "You really don't get why she left?" Maiku looked away from Miina's unbearable stare.

Is it that I really don't get it? Or am I just pretending I don't because I don't want to admit what the real reason is?

These questions pierced Maiku's heart at its weakest point. Maiku quickly shrugged them off. Those questions would have to wait. He told himself that the most important thing right now was to find Karen.

"We'll talk after we find Karen."

"I'm not going."

"What?" Maiku raised his eyebrows at Miina's surprising answer. "What do you mean you're not going? Aren't you worried about Karen?"

"Of course I'm worried!"

"Then why won't you go?"

Miina bit her lip and kept quiet. In her mind she was screaming enough to make her cough up blood.

How could I go?!

When Miina had run away because she was worried about whether or not she was related to Maiku, Karen had come after her. Then she told Miina who was afraid of losing the right to love Maiku, "Until we know for sure who is related to him I'm going to keep on loving him. I don't think we should worry about it or give up on it until we know the truth."

It was those words that made Miina realize that Karen was stronger than she looked. Karen, true to her word, continued to love Maiku. When she learned the truth, she must have been overwhelmed by her feelings that had become so strong. So she ran away. Miina, who had the same feelings, understood what Karen was going through all too well. If she had been the one to find out that she was the sister of the person she loved, and would be able to stay near him, but never act on her feelings, she would have done the same thing. So she could not go after Karen. To find Karen and bring her back here as Maiku's sister would be the same as declaring an end to her love for Maiku. As a fellow soldier on the battlefield of love, there was no way she could do that.

And if she found Karen what would she say? Isn't that great that you're Maiku's sister? Since we know you're related to him now please support my relationship with him and follow the love alliance codes. Like she could say that. She only now realized how cruel those codes were for both of them.

"Come on, answer me!" Maiku yelled in his irritation at her silence. All sorts of feelings that she could not express were running through Miina's mind. "Why? Why would you be so mean? Do you think that none of this matters to you anymore now that you know you're not related to me?" Miina was still silent so Maiku turned his back to her and said, "Well, I'm going to find her."

Maiku acted as if he was about to run out the door, but he waited a minute, as if he was waiting for Miina to say, "Wait, I'm going with you." But when Miina remained silent, he spoke again without turning to look at her.

"I'm really disappointed. I didn't think you were like this. I really thought of you like a little sister, too."

Those words were unbearably cruel for Miina. But Maiku ran down the stairs without turning around to see the pained expression on her face.

Damnit! What the hell was that all about?

Maiku impatiently put his shoes on and ran out of the house. He put on his helmet and jumped onto his scooter.

Why would Miina be like that?

Maiku wondered about Miina's incomprehensible behavior, but he left those worries behind with the sound of his engine revving as he rode off into the dark red sunset. His first priority was to find Karen. First he went to the nearest train station and looked around. Then he headed to the school, the Herikawa shop where she worked, the nearby convenience stores, and anywhere else Karen seemed likely to go. She was nowhere to be found.

Where could she have gone?

He did not even really have a clue where Karen would go. After looking at all the places he could think of, he was at a loss as to what to do next. According to what Miina said, Karen left sometime during the thirty minutes while Miina was preparing dinner. It did not look as if she took anything with her, so she probably had not gone anywhere on the train. Karen, who was slow and clumsy at everything she did, probably could not have gone far. Maiku could not just sit around and wait so he rode through the neighborhood on his scooter. His driving became wild as he was overcome with worry.

Why... why would she leave? After she finally found that she is my sister, after she found out that we are blood related.

Maiku was vaguely aware of what the answer to his question was , but he just kept driving around.

"What's this 'something cool' you're gonna show me?" Haruko asked her brother who was walking ahead, leading her down a path toward the mountains.

"You'll see when we get there," Matagu said, smiling what he thought was a friendly smile.

"Come on, just tell me!" Haruko pleaded, pouting at Matagu's remark.

"We'll be there soon."

When Matagu first asked her if she would go on a walk with him to see 'something cool' she had refused. But when Matagu would not give up, she agreed to go if he bought her ice cream. She followed him, licking the ice cream he bought her at a convenience store. She had no idea where he was taking her, but he kept heading farther and farther toward the mountains. When she had the ice cream to occupy her she had kept quiet, but when she finished it she started to regret having agreed in coming along with him.

"Are we there yet?"

If he was going to make her walk anymore she was turning back, no matter how much he protested. Then Matagu stopped where he was standing on a small path that was surrounded on either side by trees and pointed ahead of him.

"We're here, Haruko."

There was a small observatory on the clearing just past the trees.

It had a steel frame work and was about three or four meters high. It was a little bit like a summer house on stilts.

"This is supposed to be cool?" Haruko said, making a funny face.

"Yeah, go up there and look," Matagu said, pushing her forward.

At the top of the rusty stairs that went up to the elevated platform there was a landing with a triangular roof. There was only a railing surrounding the landing and the view was incredible.

"Wow!" Haruko said leaning over the railing and looking down at the scenery that was bathed in a clear orange light from the sunset.

"Isn't it beautiful, Haruko?" Matagu asked, standing next to her. Her eyes shone brightly and she nodded.

"Yeah!"

She was not expecting Matagu's idea of 'something cool' to actually be cool. She was surprised to have been brought to such a beautiful view rather than something stupid.

"This is where a friend of mine promised his love to the girl he likes."

"Really?" she was so taken away by the beauty of the view, that she was only half listening.

"Don't you think this is a really romantic place for a love confession, Haruko?"

"Yeah," she said, still not really paying attention.

"This place probably has the power to bring people together," Matagu said, moving closer to Haruko as if he was up to something.

"Oh!" Haruko suddenly raised her voice, just as Matagu was about to put his arm around her bare shoulders and pull her close to him.

Matagu jumped and pulled his arm away.

"What's wrong?"

"There's a crow."

"Huh?"

Matagu followed Haruko's look at saw several crows flying off, perhaps to go home to their nests, toward the sun that was setting behind the mountains. Haruko spun around away from the sunset as she heard the crows cawing.

"The crows are going home, we should too!"

"Wh-what?!"

Haruko did not even take notice of Matagu's panic and lightly walked down the stairs.

"Wait a minute, Haruko!" Matagu said, quickly running after his sister. "You can't go yet, not when it was just about to get good!"

Haruko looked uninterested in what her brother had to say and walked back down the path. Matagu reluctantly followed her, and as they were walking down the small incline they suddenly saw Karen appear from the trees on the left side.

"Karen!" Haruko exclaimed, surprised to see Karen. However, her surprise could not compare to that of Karen who quickly ran off in the direction she had come from, as if afraid of them.

"And she's gone…"

"What was that all about?" asked Matagu.

"I dunno."

Haruko and Matagu looked at each other after they watched Karen disappear up the hill. As they walked onto the paved road just past the wooded area, they had another strange encounter. A guy on a scooter went by them and then suddenly put on the breaks. The guy on the bike turned and looked at them, still straddling the bike. Haruko's eyes widened when she realized who it was.

"Kamishiro?"

"Have you seen Karen?" Maiku asked, without any sort of greeting.

"Yeah we saw her."

Maiku, who was not really expecting an answer, was completely caught off guard. He soon got his wits about him and asked eagerly, "Where? Where did you see her?"

Haruko was practically thrown back by his enthusiastic response, but managed to point down the path they had just come from. "Over there. She was just running toward the observatory tower over there."

Maiku got off his scooter and quickly walked toward them as he took off his helmet.

"What happened? If you'd like me to help, I'd…" said Matagu, trying to act like a mature, experienced upperclassman.

"Hold this for me," Maiku said, handing him his helmet.

"This is not what I meant by helping!" Matagu tried to protest, but Maiku was already hopping off to the observatory tower, looming like a sentinel nearby.

What's she doing here?

Of course Maiku had no way of knowing this, but after Karen left the house she wandered around aimlessly and ended up getting lost in the mountains. Since Karen herself was not even sure where she had ended up, it was not surprising that Maiku had had a hard time finding her.

As Maiku ran through the woods he felt an odd sense of deja-vu. *What is this feeling? It's so familiar...*

The girl/ with blue eyes/ and a kind face/ but all I feel is sadness/ who is she?/ the girl that I love/ on her lips/ the words 'I'm sorry'/ I'm losing sight/ of those blue eyes/ her warmth/ I don't want to lose it/ no/ no/ no...

This song was a far off memory from his childhood. Or maybe it was a made up tragedy. Before he could figure out what this song meant, he reached the end of the wooded area. He immediately saw Karen sitting on the bottom step of the stairs up to the observatory tower.

"Karen!" Maiku yelled. Karen, who had been sitting with her head hung down, quickly looked up. She stood up, as if by reflex, and turned around to run away from Maiku. But being the truly clumsy girl that she was, she tripped and fell right where she had been standing. She quickly stood up, but Maiku grabbed her by the wrist from behind.

"L-let go of me!"

"Why? Why did you leave? After you found out that you're my sister, that we're related..."

"That's why. I left because I found out I was related to you."

"What? That doesn't make any sense. What do you mean?" Maiku demanded an explanation.

"I like you!" she blurted out. She and Maiku both stopped moving, as if frozen in place by her proclamation. It felt as if the entire world had gone silent.

"So I don't want to be your sister. If I was, I could be with you, but I could never love you like I do."

Maiku slowly let go of Karen's wrist. Karen pulled back her arm that now had marks on it from being held so tightly. Karen's words seemed to have taken all the life out of Maiku and his shoulders slumped forward. The setting sun bathed the two of them in a warm red light. Maiku's lips were barely moving, as if he was trying to say something. Then, as if he had suddenly regained his strength, he made two tight fists.

"Then... then don't be my sister," Maiku said, still looking down.

"I can't just decide not to be your sister. We're related by blood, so..."

Maiku looked up and fastened his gaze on Karen. Karen was taken aback by the intensity of his look.

"It doesn't matter," Maiku interrupted her.

"What?"

"None of that matters!" Maiku said, pulling Karen close to him with both of his arms. Karen stiffened at his sudden advance on her, and he leaned his head against her neck, hugging her slight figure tightly.

"Please, Karen. Stay with me."

Karen felt something hot and wet fall on her shoulder.

Maiku's crying...

It was the first time Maiku had ever cried in front of Karen.

"I don't want to lose anybody else. I don't want to be abandoned by anybody else. Don't leave me."

"Maiku..." Karen could not bring herself to say anything else.

I'm so sorry. I was only thinking of myself.

It was so simple that she had not even realized it. Her leaving was the same as abandoning Maiku. Karen had never thought about it like that until that moment. Maiku revealing his weakest point had made her realize just how selfish she had been. Maiku squeezed her even tighter, as if he was never going to let her go again.

Karen was overjoyed that Maiku needed her so much, but at the same time it made her incredibly sad. She was sad because she needed Maiku, too, but not in the way a sister needs her bother. Their blood relation should have brought them closer together, but instead it stood between them like an insurmountable wall.

"I want to stay by your side. I always… always want to be with you. But… but…" Karen felt a lump in her throat as she started to cry. Maiku suddenly put his hands on her shoulders and pushed her away from his body. Then, with such a force that she was helpless against him, he leaned in to kiss her.

At that moment their teeth hit hard enough to make a sound. Karen's eyes widened in surprise from the sudden kiss. Her mind went blank and she could not remember whether the kiss lasted for a second, or much longer. Maiku pulled his lips away from hers.

"That's my answer," said Maiku to the stunned Karen.

And with that Karen understood his intention. He was going to move on and overcome whatever he had to.

Maiku was looking deeply into Karen's eyes. The look made her feel like he was waiting for her answer. There was no longer any doubt or hesitation in her mind. Karen stood up on her tiptoes and pressed her lips against his.

One hour before Maiku found Karen, Miina, who had been left

at home alone, was still sitting in the second floor room as if she had forgotten how to move her legs.

I'm so happy... that Maiku said he thinks of me as a sister, Miina thought and her eyes welled up with tears again. Why did this happen?

The three of them had been brought together by one picture. They had finally found happiness living together, and now that one picture had destroyed it all.

The tears rolled down Miina's cheeks and onto the picture that was sitting in front of her.

If only I hadn't found this stupid picture.

Miina was overcome by guilt as she picked up the picture. The short string of words written on the back had brought on the whole horrible situation. She wanted to look away, but she could not ignore the pain in her mind. She turned the picture over in her hands.

"Maiku and Karyn O.'s first time in the pool"

After rereading those words Miina noticed that something was not quite right. At first she did not know what it was, but as she ran her tear-filled eyes over the words again she figured it out.

Her name's spelled wrong...

It was true. Instead of 'Karen' it said 'Karyn.' The person who wrote it had to be Maiku and Karen's mother or father. The handwriting was very soft and beautiful, so most likely their mother had written it. Would a mother who had gone through the pain of childbirth really misspell her own child's name? It was possible, but Karen was a very common name. What were the chances that a mother would name her daughter 'Karen' and then accidentally write it with the less common spelling 'Karyn'? If it was someone else who had written it, it was quite possible that they might have made a mistake. So that would mean that maybe someone besides their parents wrote it. If Miina had not noticed that 'O.' after Karen's name she might have gone with that explanation. Miina realized that there could be a completely different reason for the mistake.

What if the person who wrote it was Maiku's mother, but not Karen's? Then the answer was simple. She had written 'Karyn' maybe because she knew another person who spelled their name that way, and put the 'O.' after it for her last name. Of course she would not need an initial for her own child, Maiku.

Could that really be true, though?

Miina was overwhelmed by the possibility of her own theory. If she were right, that would mean that the two children in the picture were not brother and sister. She kept thinking as she held back the urge to yell out loud.

Why had she assumed that the children in the picture were related? The main reason was probably that they both had blue eyes. But even more importantly than that objective fact, it might have been the hope that somewhere she had a sibling. Maiku and Karen no doubt felt the same. But what if that was another mistake, like the assumption that the house in the picture was where the children had grown up?

Soon Miina was holding the picture so tightly that it began to crease.

I've got to find out…

As she wiped away her tears and stood up, Miina recalled the place where she had found the picture. It was lying in front of a partially opened closet in a worn-out Japanese-style room. It looked as if it had fallen from inside the closet. That would mean there might be more pictures inside the closet. There might even be a picture that would tell her once and for all whether those two blue-eyed children were related or not.

Miina went downstairs, put on her shoes and went out the door. The sun had not completely set, but the eastern sky was now a deep purple. She would need a flashlight to search the deserted house now. She went back into the house and got a flashlight. She held it in one hand and crossed the street, heading toward the deserted house she had hoped never to enter again. Bathed in the dim light of the sunset, the half-decaying house looked even more foreboding than in the daytime. If she had not had firm determination, she would never have been able to convince herself to go inside.

Miina went inside and turned on the flashlight. She pointed it on the ground in front of her and headed to the room on the second floor where she had found the picture. The footprints she had left in the dust in the hall were quite visible. She found it hard to breathe, not because of the stuffy air, but rather because of her own nerves.

Miina stood before the closet and pushed the broken door all the way open. Immediately all the various items that were shoved into the bottom shelf of the closet came spilling out. It seemed that whoever had lived her before had not been very good at organizing. Miina coughed violently as dust rose off of the pile. When she managed to stop coughing, she pointed the flashlight on the pile of stuff. The white circle of light caught an old notebook. It said "Baby Book" in the same handwriting that was on the back of the picture. Miina's heart was pounding as she picked up the book and opened it. On the first page it said...

"A record of the growth of my two adorable children -- Maiku and Miina"

It was already pitch black outside by the time Maiku and Karen got home. Karen's clothes had mud stains on them from when she fell down trying to run away from Maiku and she must have gotten a scratch because she had a little bit of blood on her sock. They both looked very serious. Miina greeted them so casually that she almost sounded disappointed to see them.

"So you're finally home?" Miina had poked her head around the corner when she heard the sound of the door opening. "You're all muddy! You should go get in the bath, it's all ready for you," she said when she noticed Karen's appearance.

Karen felt relieved that Miina did not ask her any questions, and walked around her to go to the bathroom. She must have hurt her leg when she fell because she had a small limp. Maiku stood in the entrance-way looking at Miina like he was waiting for her to say something.

"I've got to talk to you, Maiku."

Maiku nodded silently and followed Miina into the sitting room. The baby book and several pictures Miina had found at the deserted house were lying on the table. Miina sat down by the table and after Maiku sat down across from her, she pushed the book toward him. Maiku took the book and looked at her like he wanted to ask something.

"I found this at…" Miina paused, "…at our real house."

Maiku gulped and looked down at the writing on the cover of the book.

"So this is…"

"I'll explain in a minute, just look at the first page."

Maiku opened the book as she told him to and looked down at

the first page. As soon as he saw what was written he looked up. He looked at Miina with his eyes wide.

"Miina, this is…"

Miina licked her lips and told him everything about how she found the book. Maiku silently listened to her entire story. He finally opened his mouth after she was completely finished explaining.

"So… so that would mean that my sister... the one who's related to me is…"

"Me," Miina said, looking Maiku in the eyes.

"Then what about Karen?"

"I think that she probably lived in the house across the street… that is, this house."

"Is that written in here?" Maiku asked, pointing to the book. He had still only looked at the first page.

"I haven't looked inside the book yet. I thought the three of us should read it together," Miina said, shaking her head. "These were stuck in the baby book," Miina said, pushing the pictures on the table toward Maiku. There were several pictures all of Maiku and the others as children and all with a short note written on the back in permanent marker. There was one picture of two young girls sleeping next to each other and on the back it said, "Miina napping with Karyn O. from across the street." The person who had written these notes always spelled Karen's name as 'Karyn.'

"So Karen lived across the street from us…" Maiku did not seem able to take it all in yet and he kept staring at the pictures with an unfocused gaze.

"So I'm your sister, and Karen is not related to you at all. Do you get it?" Miina said, trying to put it simply for him. Maiku nodded awkwardly and Miina got up enthusiastically to end the conversation. "I'm going to go take a bath. I've got to tell Karen everything."

"Yeah, you should," Maiku said in a cracked voice.

"I'm coming in," Miina said playfully as she went into the bathroom. Karen was sitting in the tub with her legs pulled stiffly up against her naked body. After Miina had poured a bucket of water over her body to rinse off, she slid into the tub with Karen. Miina cleared her throat obviously and looked at Karen who was slumped forward.

"Um, in accordance with the second code of the love alliance, I, Miina Miyafuji, would like to report that I am related to Maiku by blood."

Karen looked up with confusion at Miina.

"And further, I, Miina Miyafuji, will implement the third code and promise to support the relationship of Maiku Kamashiro and Karen Onodera from this day…"

"Miina!" Karen could not take it anymore and she yelled so loud that it echoed through the room. "What are you talking about? Aren't I the one who is related to…"

"Nope," Miina said without listening to the rest of the question. She explained everything to Karen just as she had to Maiku. When she finished Karen looked stunned.

"That's how it is. Got it?"

Karen nodded, but without the proof of the baby book and pictures she was finding it a little hard to believe. Miina sighed and repeated exactly what she had said to Maiku.

"So I'm Maiku's sister and you are not related to him at all."

Miina got out of the bathtub and wrapped a towel around her naked body and went to the door of the sitting room where she thought Maiku would be.

"The bath's free!" she called to him.

"Thanks, I'll use it later." Maiku's voice sounded a bit far away because he was out on the front porch. "And Miina? Once you get your pajamas on can you and Karen both come here?"

"Yeah, sure."

Miina went up the stairs after Karen, wondering what Maiku was doing out there. Miina and Karen went down to the porch outside the sitting room after they had changed into their pajamas. Maiku, who was standing outside by the clothes line, had lit a bonfire. He had filled a barrel full of old newspapers and they were burning intensely.

"Why are you making a fire on such a hot day?" Miina said, asking the obvious question. Maiku picked up the baby book that was sitting on the porch.

"I was thinking I'd burn this," Maiku said casually. Miina and Karen looked shocked. "I haven't read it yet."

"So you want to just burn it without even reading it?" Miina said, louder than she meant to.

"Yeah. We already found out what we wanted to know."

"But there's a lot written about our childhood in there! There might even be something about our family, maybe even why we were abundoned and…"

"That stuff doesn't matter," Maiku said, curtly. "At least, it doesn't matter to me anymore. Up until now I had always wanted to know who my parents were, where I was born, where I lived, and why I was abandoned. I sat around thinking about it all the time. I tried to forget about it, but it was always there in my mind." A smile crept across Maiku's face. He seemed to be smiling at himself. "But now I know," Maiku glanced at Karen. "I know that the past doesn't matter. I don't even remember, so why do I need to know? What's important now is the present... and the future."

Miina looked at the calm, yet determined expression on Maiku's face and let her shoulders relax.

"Yeah. You're right, Maiku."

"So I can..." Maiku started to ask.

"Yeah. I think you should burn it," Miina said, nodding.

"What do you think, Karen?"

"I think you should do it," Karen answered surprisingly without any hesitation.

"Then let's do it," Miina said. Maiku looked from Miina's face to Karen's to confirm their agreement and threw the baby book into the flames. The book was instantly engulfed by the flames, and one key to their pasts burned up and a wisp of smoke wafted up into the star-filled sky.

That night, Karen could not fall asleep after she climbed into her futon. She was still worked up about all that had happened that day. She should have been tired, but her eyes were still wide open.

"Hey Karen?" Miina said softly in the dark from the futon next to Karen. She could not sleep either. "Are you still awake?"

"Yes, I can't get to sleep."

"Me neither," Miina said looking up at the ceiling through the darkness. "It's weird, isn't it?"

"What is?"

"That I'm Maiku's sister," Miina said. Karen stiffened under her thin summer blanket. "So that means, if you marry Maiku you'd be my sister."

"You're getting ahead of yourself, Miina!"

"We'd be sisters-in-law!"

"Come on! Don't tease me like that!" Karen said, puffing out her cheeks. Miina climbed into Karen's futon, as if maybe she wanted to poke her cheeks. "Wh-what are you doing, Miina?!"

Miina hugged the upset Karen, leaning her head against her chest.

"Karen, if you were my sister you'd comfort me, right? Just for a bit?" Miina felt a lump in her throat like she was going to cry. She stayed in Karen's futon and her shoulders lightly quivered as she cried silently.

"Miina…" Karen's heart filled with intense emotion. But she did not cry. She desperately held back her tears. She knew that now was not her turn to cry. She put her arms around Miina and held her tenderly.

Epilogue: And Then There Were Three...

Karen sighed heavily as she walked along the road along the lake after the end of the first semester.

"That's the thirteenth time you've sighed, Karen," said Miina rolling her eyes as she walked on Karen's right side. She must have been counting them for her.

"Were your grades really that bad?" asked Maiku who was on her left side.

"It's a catastrophe," said Karen looking at him with a long face.

"Don't get so down about it. It's in the past now," Miina said indifferently. Maiku looked at Miina over Karen's hanging head.

"And how did you do, may I ask?"

"Me? Well, uh, probably about the same as Karen," Miina said and quickly added, "But it's OK. I don't care anyway."

"Maybe you should care!"

"What's the point of worrying about it? You know what they say, 'regret comes too late.'"

"And I'm saying you should regret it!"

They were still bickering when their house came into sight.

"Well, how about I regret it later, and for a change of pace we go somewhere tomorrow?" Miina suggested, in her carefree manner.

"No," Maiku refused flatly.

"Awww, why not?" Miina asked, pouting.

"I've got a lot of work to do."

"But it's summer vacation. Can't you take one day off to have fun?"

"It's because I've been goofing off too much recently that I'm so busy now."

"Come on!" Miina pleaded, and grabbed Maiku's arm, practically pushing Karen away. Miina pushed her developing, immature body covered in white light summer clothes into Maiku. "It's summer vacation! We should go somewhere!"

"M-Miina!" Karen yelled in a high, shaky voice at Miina's bold pestering.

"What?" Miina said, looking at Karen innocently.

"Isn't… isn't that against the love alliance codes?"

"Of course not! I'm just being close to my beloved big brother!" Miina said, and with that Karen went around to Maiku's other side and grabbed his free arm. She clung to him tightly, not to be outdone by Miina.

"Hey, come on, you guys…" Maiku looked troubled with Miina and Karen grabbing onto him from both sides. He tried to wriggle away from them saying, "Cut it out!"

"Nope! We won't let you go until you promise to take us somewhere," Miina said.

"We're not letting go," Karen said, nodding in agreement. Maiku was stuck between the two of them who were suddenly working together against him.

"Fine, I'll take you somewhere. That's all I have to do, right?" Maiku finally answered.

"Yay!" Karen and Miina both yelled happily at the same time. But neither of them let go of Maiku's arms, as if they had forgotten what they said just before.

They sky was clear and blue. The sunlight danced and sparkled on the lake. A cool breeze blew through the big trees that looked like upside-down umbrellas. Just where the road that wound along the lake turned off onto the unpaved road, the three kids stood together in a clump. This was the beginning of Maiku Kamishiro, Karen Onodera, and Miina Miyafuji's summer vacation.

THE END

Afterword by Go Zappa

Hi everyone. Welcome back old fans, and welcome new fans! I'm Zappa. I find myself as a sort of Chris Spedding of the young adult fiction word, when I was hoping to be a "Kootch". Or even better, it would be nice to be like Ian McLagan. But I guess you don't care about that.

So, how did you like the novelization of the popular anime Onegai Twins? Instead of novelization, I suppose this is more like another version of the original (just like the alternate paths in dating simulation games). Rather than an exact copy of the original, it just keeps the general story and some of the characters are different than those who appear in the anime, and there are some new ones, and some who didn't end up in the anime show up in the novel (for example, I personally really like XXX and I was really mad she wasn't in the anime, so I used my power as the author and put her in anyway. LOL). I guess some of the hardcore fans will be annoyed, but please try to forgive me and I hope you will read the next OneTwi book.

I was offered the chance to do the novel version by Yosuke Kuroda, who is in charge of the series organization, because I had done the novel version of Onegai Teacher, the basis for Onegai Twins. When he showed me the scenario for the anime, I thought it seemed like it would be difficult to do, but then the anime started airing and I thought it was really incredible, so I felt pressure to do the book. So at first I kind of had stars in my eyes (that's an old phrase!) after having seen this great anime, but after that I just felt really pressured and I slowly worked at it everyday, for better or for worse. I especially spent a long time thinking about the ending and how I should bring it all together. I was actually so worried that I didn't even eat a decent meal and just survived on snacks. I think you could call it a miracle (though there are some that might disagree with me) that I even finished on schedule. If it hadn't been for the practically free ride the people from the anime production group were giving me, I probably would have given up and run away from the hard work. Who knows, by now I could have changed my name and been at some hot springs resort in Atami secretly working as the guy in charge of watching people's shoes.

Well, let's forget about all that for now. I put all of my efforts into making this novel the best it could be, so what happens now is of no concern to me... no, no, I mean I'm waiting to hear what everyone thinks and feeling a bit like a fish waiting on the cutting board.

Finally, I would like to thank Mr. Kuroda for asking me to do this and not holding my erotic novelization of Onegai Teacher against me -- Taraku Uon and Hiroaki Goda for taking the time to draw the great illustrations, various members of the elite anime staff, including Yasunori Ide who was kind enough to write commentary for this book, the great voice actors for OneTwi (particularly Mai Nakahara and Ai Shimizu who gave me comments, Shouro Miura... correction, Hiroaki Miura, who gave me great inspiration through his interpretation of Matagu Shido), Hideyuki Kurata who agreed to write commentary on the first book, and the editors at Dengeki Publishing who patiently waited for the manuscript. Thank you all!

So I hope to see you all again when the third book, Onegai Twins: The Threesome, comes out. (Just kidding!)

P.S. If you're interested please check out my website.

Zappa Hermitage:

http://www007.upp.so-net.ne.jp/zappa-an/

Written while listening to 'Karen in Love' by Eiichi Oota.

Commentary
Yasunori Ide (Director of Onegai Twins)

Go Zappa is not just any guy. He brought something that was sure, yet unsure, to life here. I cried several times when I read this book. I could never read it in front of anyone. It should be read alone, quietly and solemnly. Then you get even more caught up in the story and are more emotionally affected. And that is tremendously annoying.

If you've reached the point that you are reading this commentary, then I think you know more than well enough how wonderful this book is and there is no need for me to spend too much time on that. I would rather tell you a little more about the Onegai Series.

The series is based around the theme of youth, something that's a bit rare these days. Perhaps it has that theme because the director (me) is really obsessed with youth. Even looking back a while, there are few great original works on the theme. Entering the field presented a challenge, but at the same time a great risk. The biggest risk was that it was an original work. In order to compensate for the fact that it was an unknown, we tried to bring in and implement as many ideas as possible. We stood ready in the 'offensive' position.

I wouldn't be exaggerating if I said the Onegai Series was a series of challenges coming at us. It was quite the opposite of the easy-going rhythm that the series itself has. In these three years the people who came together, the people who left, all worked together to achieve something amazing. It is deeply moving to look back at all we did. Having just finished reading this book, I feel like we have accomplished something again. This novel made real all the things that we could not include in the anime version.

Through the novels, we have achieved the real feeling we were aiming for. I think we've done enough. I think we can move on to the next thing. This book gave me the solace to be able to naturally think that. There is a comfortable weight in my hands. I am deeply grateful to be able to feel this way, grateful to Mr. Zappa, and to Maiku and the girls.

Maiku, Miina, and Karen struggle. They struggle to live their lives. From an adult's point of view, each step they take is as uncertain as the one before. But they are living for now. They are looking ahead to tomorrow. I can still learn something from them. I can learn what I have to do…